A GRIM ALMANAC OF

CORNWALL

JOHN VAN DER KISTE

The History Press

First published 2009

The History Press
The Mill, Brimscombe Port
Stroud, Gloucestershire, GL5 2QG
www.thehistorypress.co.uk

British Library Cataloguing in Publication Data.
A catalogue record for this book is available from the British Library.

ISBN 978 0 7509 5131 9

Typesetting and origination by The History Press
Printed in Great Britain

CONTENTS

ALSO BY
JOHN VAN DER KISTE

AUTHOR'S NOTE AND ACKNOWLEDGEMENTS

Cornwall can boast a rich tapestry of dark history to compare with that of any other county in England. Murders, suicides, fatal mining accidents, fires, explosions, shipwrecks and severe weather disasters have all taken their toll of the less fortunate. In the sixteenth and seventeenth centuries religious conflicts, notably the Prayer Book Rebellion, and the persecution of Roman Catholics and Quakers, left their mark on the county, to say nothing of battles during the Civil War. Ghost stories, superstition, witchcraft and even cannibalism have also featured in Cornwall's past. All these appear in the following pages, and I hope this journey through the ages will prove as rewarding to those who read it as it was for me to research and write it. I have also included a few tales from the Isles of Scilly, which have had a unitary authority since 1889, although they have traditionally been administered, and are historically regarded, as part of the county of Cornwall.

Whilst doing so I have had the benefit of a variety of books, journals and websites. I would also like to acknowledge the help of Nicola Sly, Phil Wright, Barry Hodges, Tony Atkin, Neil Clifton, Kevin Hale, Brian, Trevor Rickard and Christine Matthews for their help with photographing various locations, and to Phil for suggesting ideas and subjects for inclusion which I would otherwise have missed. Anna and John Coles were also a mine of information in answering questions on Cornish history which proved difficult to solve elsewhere. Local history collections at the libraries at Truro, Plymouth and Exeter have also been invaluable repositories of information for the subject.

Last but not least, as ever, my wife Kim has been a tower of strength in her constant support and encouragement from the start of writing through to the reading of the final manuscript, as well as ever ready to help with the photography, while my editors at The History Press, Matilda Richards and Beth Amphlett, have been tireless in seeing the work through to publication. My heartfelt thanks are due to all.

JANUARY

Tregothnan, a house and estate beside the village of St Michael Penkivel, near Truro. It was the traditional home of Lord Falmouth, whose gamekeeper was murdered there on 26 January 1904.

St Michael's Mount.

1 JANUARY 1896

Fisherman John Tenbeth left his home in the afternoon to go out in his boat in the direction of St Michael's Mount, but he failed to return. Next afternoon some wreckage, later identified as part of his boat, was picked up on the Eastern Green. His body was never recovered. He left a widow and several children.

2 JANUARY 1852

SS *Amazon*, sailing from Southampton to the West Indies on her maiden voyage, was lost off the Scilly Isles, and 115 of the 161 passengers and crew on board were killed. She had run into a strong headwind in the English Channel and her engine bearings had become red-hot through unexpected friction, forcing her to be brought to a standstill twice. During the worst of the storm, while trying to pick up speed, a fire broke out in front of one of her twin funnels and the flames quickly spread. The passengers tried to launch the lifeboats, but only a small proportion of those on board managed to sail to safety. Within a few hours the ship was ablaze and, after two explosions, what still remained of the ship sank to the bottom of the sea, with Captain William Symons and most of his crew and passengers still on board.

Most of those who were lucky enough to escape were spotted by a brig which landed them at Falmouth. Midshipman James Vincent, who commanded one of the few boats which succeeded in getting clear, later spoke of himself and fellow survivors looking back towards the ship and seeing people on the decks, some of whom were kneeling quietly in prayer, while others were running about and

The SS Amazon
*was lost off
the Isles Scilly
in 1852, with
the loss of 115
passengers and
crew.*

screaming in their terror. At the subsequent enquiry Vincent spoke of the nine lifeboats with which *Amazon* was fitted, mentioning that four were secured in such a way that launching them would have been impossible. He also said that at no stage did the captain give orders to abandon ship; his only words as he had watched the inferno were, 'It is all over with her.'

3 JANUARY 1952

Francis Gordon Wilson, of Avondale Road, Truro, an employee at the Truro Income Tax Offices, collapsed and died in Reed's chemists, Francis Street, Truro.

4 JANUARY 1905

An inquest at the Royal Sisters Home, Falmouth, was held into the death of Matthew Wallace (40), master of Cardiff steamer *Gloxinia*. He had gone to bed after breakfast on 2 January at 11 a.m. coughing badly and saying his indigestion was making him feel ill. He had taken some bicarbonate of soda in the hope that this would relieve the problem. The steward, Robert Henderson, gave him mustard emetic, then Wallace told him he would prefer to be left alone. Henderson returned to look in on him at 1 p.m. and then went to fetch the chief officer and engineer, as Wallace had a blue-yellow tint to his face and Henderson was anxious about him. They confirmed that Wallace was dead. Dr Bullmore held the post-mortem and established that death was due to the congested state of blood vessels of the heart, though he could not say what had been the cause.

5 JANUARY 1904

An explosion at the National Explosives Company near Hayle at about 10.45 a.m. killed four men and injured several others. The men were working in buildings used for mixing nitro-glycerine. Two of the buildings, 60yds apart, were blown to pieces and 'the remains of the men were scattered in all directions.' The air was filled with dense clouds of smoke and dust, and the impact was felt several miles away. In St Ives shop-fronts were damaged and windows fell into the streets, the roads were covered with shattered glass, and an elderly woman went into a coma for several hours through either fright or shock.

At the inquest into the deaths the following week, it was concluded that the accident was probably caused by one of the lids of the tanks being raised to see how the tank was filling and being accidentally dropped, knocking the nitro-glycerine and thus causing the explosion.

6 JANUARY 1942

An inquest was held at Falmouth into the death of Lieutenant Alan Morell (29) of Windsor, a subaltern in the Duke of Cornwall's Light Infantry. While riding his motorcycle on Longdowns Road, Penryn, he somersaulted twice over the handlebars and was killed instantly. Mr Shallish told the

The Hayle National Explosives Company was the scene of a fatal explosion in 1904.

Penryn.

County Coroner, Mr L.J. Carlyon, that he was driving from Truro to Helston when Morell passed him at a speed of 45mph. About 200yds in front of Morell was a civilian lorry driver, Mr Mabe, who put his right hand out to indicate a right turn. Morell tried to pass him, and the lorry was almost across the road before Morell applied his brakes. He went over the handlebars, but the cycle did not strike the lorry. Mabe said he saw the motorcycle skid when the officer applied his brakes and saw Morell turn two somersaults. The coroner said that Mr Mabe had given reasonable signal of his intention to turn. The deceased had been going at high speed on a straight road, but unfortunately did not see the signal in time, and had applied his brakes too suddenly.

7 JANUARY 1861

William Phillips (50), a cooper who lived at St Austell, told his son he was going out to shoot some small birds in the adjoining fields. Earlier, he had complained of feeling indisposed. When he came back, he was climbing up a ladder against the house when his gun exploded and some shot was lodged in his chest. His son heard the noise and went out to investigate. Phillips said, 'I'm shot,' and his son ran to fetch the surgeon, Mr J. Pearce. However, by the time the latter appeared, Phillips was dead. He left a widow and four children.

Fore Street, St Austell.

8 JANUARY 1914

Mr W.J. Kelynack (51), sub-postmaster in High Street, Penzance, died of heart failure in Birmingham while he was on his honeymoon. A widower, he had recently married Miss Arberry in the Penzance United Methodist Church on 5 January, but had been in poor health since Christmas. In his younger days he had been well known as a cricketer for the town club, and had sometimes captained the team.

9 JANUARY 1940

An inquest was held on the bodies of Beatrice (50) and James Wills (58), a miner, who had both lived at Goonlaze. Beatrice was found dead on 4 January with severe head injuries caused by a blunt instrument. There were no signs of any struggle, and a hammer was found nearby. Her husband had cut his throat.

Janie Williams, James's niece, told the inquest that she had gone out shopping on 4 January when her uncle saw her and called to her to 'come quickly'. He gave her two bunches of keys and two purses, and asked her to give them to his adopted son. He had been a widower when he married Beatrice in February 1939 and Janie said she was aware they 'had difficulties', but she did not know what had caused them. A fortnight earlier Beatrice had left him and a housekeeper had moved in, but she only stayed a couple of days before his wife returned.

James Williams of Goonown, the adopted son, said he thought they had been quite happy, and did not know of any quarrels. On 3 January both of them seemed perfectly cheerful. On 4 January he went to the house, looked through the window and saw somebody on the floor. Two days later he came to the house again and saw Mr Wills, who said his wife was dead. Then somebody knocked on the door and he disappeared out the back. The witness asked him what he was going to do, and he said he was intending to give himself up before the day was out.

Constable James said he knew the couple well, and they frequently quarrelled and separated for short periods. During the last month they had often called at the police station with domestic complaints. Wills was of a very jealous disposition, and often complained of his wife's association with other men. She grumbled about his jealousy, and had said she was going to apply for a summons of separation. James Wills' body was found on 6 January in a meadow. His throat had been cut and there was a razor in his hand. Verdicts were returned of murder and suicide while of unsound mind.

10 JANUARY 1930

Leonard Bassett (42) was riding in his cart on his farm near Mevagissey, when some brambles touched the horse, causing it bolted. He sprang off the cart and ran beside it for about 70yds. A neighbouring farmer, Joseph Wills, had been watching and came to help. By the time he reached them the horse was lying on its side, and the shaft of the cart was on Bassett's neck. Wills was unable to free the injured man on his own, and by the time he was able to summon three others to assist, Bassett was dead. Dr Ross, who conducted the post-mortem, said that the cause of death was a broken neck.

11 JANUARY 1947

Harold Wotton of Ladock was fined £1 with 1 guinea advocate's fee at West Powder Sessions, Truro, for obtaining 8¾cwt of pig meal without proper authority. Mr R. Money, defending, said the case had come about as the result of some evil-minded person writing an anonymous letter to the authorities. The Chairman of the Magistrates, Mr W. Goodfellow, said the Bench deplored the writing of anonymous letters in any shape or form, and regretted that it should have taken place in this instance.

12 JANUARY 1898

Mrs Catherine Bullock was found dead by her husband Thomas. She was hanging from a beam in a cattle shed by a rope normally used to tie up cattle in Trewolla, St Enoder, after suffering from depression for some time.

13 JANUARY 1925

Edwin Atkinson, of the Miner's Arms, Church Street, Camborne, was fined 10s by East Penwith Magistrates' Court for selling liquor to a girl aged 13½ for consumption by her mother off the premises. Constable Stone said he saw the child leave with a bottle in her basket, and the stopper could easily be removed. The witness admitted the offence but said he had thought she was over the age limit.

14 JANUARY 1960

County pathologist Dr Denis Hocking received a call from Assistant Chief Constable Rowland, saying that two elderly ladies had been found dead in their home in Gunnislake. It was a dwelling converted from stables, with an upper floor reached by a ladder, and it was infested by rats and other vermin. The residents, two spinster sisters, Hannah (85) and Mary (94) Sullivan, were lying dead on the floor of the downstairs room. Mary had been dead for about a fortnight, her body had been thrown behind the door, and furniture placed over her – possibly a crude form of burial. On top of the pile was a wooden stool, with a cracked seat. In the crack was a white hair, similar to those on Mary's head. There was a fairly severe bruise on the left side of the forehead above the hair line, but the skin had not been broken and there was no sign of bleeding. Similar bruising was clearly visible around the left eye and over the left cheek, but no bones had been broken and no apparent damage done to the brain. The weight of the blow was thought insufficient to cause death, although it could have produced unconsciousness, and in the prevailing cold it could easily have resulted in her death from exposure.

It was thought possible that they might have had a quarrel, after which Hannah hit her sister over the head with a stool, and, thinking she was dead, had then in a panic 'buried' her under the furniture, leaving her to die of cold and exposure. Hannah had died sometime later, slumped on the floor before the fireplace, with her head in the ashes, and a thin blanket had been pulled over her body.

Upstairs, in what served as the bedroom with worn old blankets, but no mattresses, with the floor deep in rat and mouse droppings, were boxes crammed full of pound notes, and deeds of property in Ireland. Some of the documents suggested that these ladies living in the most squalid, poverty-stricken premises imaginable may have been distantly related to the Irish

New Bridge, Gunnislake.

aristocracy. Hocking thought that both women probably died of general senile degeneration, accelerated by cold and exposure.

15 JANUARY 1869

Stephen Wesley (29) of Chacewater was working in a winze (an inclined or vertical shaft or passage between the levels in a mine) at East Wheal Meade, part of St Day United Mines. He had bored a hole and was pouring in water, pressing it down lightly with the end of an iron tamping bar, when there was an explosion. The bar was blown through his head, and he was killed instantly. He left a widow and three children, one of which was just six days old.

16 JANUARY 1946

Florence Bennetts of Trelawney Road, St Ives, was brought up in custody before the town magistrates, charged with writing a threatening letter on 17 March 1942 and demanding twenty coupons from Mrs Olive Banfield. She was further charged with having on the same date sent a threatening letter, demanding money and clothing coupons, to Mrs Clara Nicholls. The court remanded her on bail.

17 JANUARY 1904

The three-masted Fowey schooner *Jasper*, owned by Richard Hockin of Newquay and laden with china clay, was wrecked on Haisborough Sands, off the Norfolk coast. Four members of crew were landed safely, but Ordinary Seaman Charles Lundberg died of exposure.

18 JANUARY 1941

Phillip Penberthy (57) of St Ives was working on the roof at Hampton Island Works, St Ives, when he fell and received multiple injuries. Although taken straight to West Cornwall Hospital, Penzance, he died shortly after admission. During the First World War he had served in the Royal Naval Reserve.

19 JANUARY 1643

A brief battle, regarded as little more than a skirmish, was fought at Braddock Down during the English Civil War. Sir Ralph Hopton, commander of the Royalist forces in the South West, had tried to raise further support in

Devon for King Charles, but the Parliamentary forces were in the ascendant and their commander, Lord Ruthin, had forced him to retreat back into Cornwall.

Hopton's army had camped the previous night at Boconnoc, and while breaking camp next morning, their vanguard of dragoons encountered the Parliamentarian cavalry already on the east side of Braddock Down. Ruthin had been too eager to wait for reinforcements under the Earl of Stamford to arrive at Liskeard; convinced that it would be an easy victory for which he could claim the credit, he intended to challenge the Royalist army on his own. In numerical terms his cavalry was superior, but Hopton had more infantry as well as two light cannon.

After two hours of long-range musket fire, with neither side willing to abandon their positions, Hopton decided to attack and ordered a general advance. They charged the Parliamentarians with such force that the latter fled after only firing a single volley which killed two men, the only Royalist casualties. Once the fugitives had reached Liskeard, the townsmen turned on them while the victorious royal forces killed around 200 men and captured a further 1,500, as well as a large amount of armaments. By the standards of most battles of the day the death toll was surprisingly light, though the result was a serious, if temporary, setback for the Parliamentary cause.

There is some dispute as to the precise site of the battle. Some historians consider it to have taken place on the East Downs, while others maintain it was fought further south.

20 JANUARY 1912

A man who gave his name as Lucien Rivers, although also known as James Burns, Deville and Wells, appeared at Falmouth Police Court charged under an extradition warrant with obtaining money by false pretences from the French government. He said that he was the man who had gained notoriety some years earlier as 'the man who broke the bank at Monte Carlo'. For the last few months he had been living under the alias of M. Deville on a small yacht in Falmouth harbour. The police also took into custody a woman, Jeanne Pairis, aged about 40, who was living with him aboard the boat.

Rivers allegedly set up an establishment at the Place Boieldieu, Paris, a building named La Rente Bimenseulle, from where he offered to pay interest at the rate of 1 per cent per day on all money sent to him for investment. People sent funds from all over France, and after he had been carrying on this business for about eight months, in April 1912, having obtained about 3,000,000 francs (equivalent to £120,000), he suddenly disappeared.

His yacht was found to be comfortably fitted and well equipped with appliances for fishing, his regular hobby. He told the magistrates that he could not deny his identity, but he felt obliged to protest against extradition, as he was an Englishman. (Which identity 'he could not deny' is open to question, although the account of his court appearance in the press the following week referred to him as Wells.) He and Pairis were remanded to Bow Street for further proceedings.

21 JANUARY 1895

Two fishermen were drowned when a number of small fishing boats went to sea off the coast of St Ives to procure bait for line fishing. Suddenly the wind veered round to the north-east and the whole fleet were caught in a severe storm. Seven or eight of the larger boats reached harbour safely. One boat, containing John Stevens (60), William Veal (25), and his younger brother Henry, tried to follow, but their craft capsized about 100yds from the beach, and before the eyes of a large number of spectators. The three men were seen clinging to the bottom of the boat, but Stevens and William Veal were soon washed off. The crowd on the beach joined hands to form a lifeline and managed to reach Stevens, who was soon picked up. The boat was washed up on the beach and Henry Veal was taken off alive. Stevens was dead, and the body of William Veal was never recovered.

22 JANUARY 1956

Mr A. Treneer (64) was found dead in bed in his cottage at St Mary's, Isles of Scilly. Mr Guy, a neighbour, had received no answer when he knocked on the door, so he went to inform Treneer's brother and the police, who came and

Workers at St Ives harbour.

entered the premises and found the body. The resident physician, Dr Bell, did a post-mortem at St Mary's Hospital and found that death was due to coronary thrombosis. It was decided there was no need for an inquest. The deceased had served with the infantry in India in the 1914–18 war, and was later employed by the Isles of Scilly Steamship Company.

23 JANUARY 1939

After a fierce gale a small sailing ketch was found flung up by the tide in Trevail Cove, three miles west of St Ives, and the bodies of two men were found nearby. A lifeboat was called out at 2.30 a.m., but conditions were very difficult as a violent north-north-west gale was blowing with wind velocity of 90mph. It had only gone about a mile when it capsized and was thrown onto a beach at Gwithian, near Godrevy Lighthouse, with the loss of seven more men.

Local fishermen said afterwards that this lifeboat and a similar one which capsized the previous year (*see* 31 January) were totally unsuited to the peculiar conditions prevailing along that part of the coast. Captain Thomas, father of John Thomas, one of the crew members who had perished, said they were prepared to risk their lives, but not to throw them away.

Colonel Satterthwaite, secretary of the Royal National Lifeboat Institution (RNLI), said that dependents of the crew would be pensioned by the institution on the same scale as if the men had been soldiers, sailors or airmen killed in battle, and a fund to be launched by the Mayor of St Ives would supplement these pensions. He endorsed the remarks of Captain Thomas, agreeing that there had to be a lifeboat adapted to meet the character of the existing conditions, while stressing that St Ives was a very important station, 'and the coast is one of the most difficult we have to handle.'

Telegrams came in from all over England expressing appreciation of the gallantry displayed by the men who lost their lives. One was from George, Duke of Kent and president of the RNLI, who had met five of the men

Gwithian beach. (© Trevor Rickard)

who lost their lives when they were decorated with the institution's medal the previous year. At the inquest on 25 January, the town mayor said he considered a breakwater was 'absolutely necessary' at the harbour, and the local authorities had been lobbying for one for nearly a hundred years.

24 JANUARY 1957

An extensive search for Gerald Woolerton, of Boyton, Launceston, a farmer who had vanished while duck shooting on 21 January, lasted for two days. On the third day it was called off, and it was assumed that he had been killed the day he went missing.

25 JANUARY 1920

The bodies of Laura Sara (40) and Joseph Hoare (57) were discovered with severe head injuries by a neighbour outside their smallholding at Skinner's Bottom, near Redruth. First aid was administered and a doctor was called, but within a couple of hours both had died. Hoare was a farmer and cattle dealer, while Sara was his housekeeper and lover, and had been separated from her husband for several years. Both were considered to be of somewhat loose morals and with a fondness for drink, and she had previously been convicted of keeping a disorderly house in Truro. The blunt instrument which had killed them was assumed to have been a bloodstained log from the pile near the cottage.

Despite intensive investigations, the killer was never found and nobody was ever charged with the murders. It was thought that attempted robbery might have been the motive, though substantial amounts of cash remained undisturbed in the cottage. At the inquest Chief Inspector Heldon of Scotland Yard advanced his theory that they may have had a violent argument and come to blows, with each being responsible for inflicting severe wounds on the other. However, the finding of only one bloodstained weapon made this seem unlikely. A more probable scenario was that somebody had lain in wait for Hoare and attacked him, Sara had gone to the door to see what the noise was about and was then killed so she would not be able to inform on the assailant.

26 JANUARY 1904

The body of Henry Osmond, a gamekeeper employed by Lord Falmouth, was found in a covert on his lordship's estate at Tregothnan. He had been killed by a single gunshot. Robert Bullen, the man suspected of the crime, was brought to the court in an ambulance. Witnesses spoke of the movements of both men on the previous day, and of a confession Bullen made to a local surgeon who was called in to dress a gunshot wound from which he was suffering. He said that Osmond had shot at him and that he fired in return, but did not know whether he had hit Osmond. The jury returned a verdict of wilful murder against Bullen, who was committed for trial.

27 JANUARY 1830

The body of Grace Andrew, an elderly woman of Calenick, near Truro, was discovered in a pool of blood in her kitchen, having been stabbed to death. Her husband was employed in the local smelting house. At an inquest held the following afternoon, it was concluded that she must have carried her husband's earnings around with her all the time, and that the murderer had killed her in order to steal the money.

In March three people living under the same roof were taken into custody on suspicion of murder, but were released after questioning. Shortly afterwards Peter Matthews, a mason from Calenick, was arrested and charged with the crime. He protested his innocence, and after lengthy investigation he appeared at Launceston Assizes on 22 March 1832 before Mr Justice Park. Evidence was given against him, but he maintained that much of it was given by members of the Skewes family with whom he had lodged, and who had a grievance against him as a result of certain financial issues. He was acquitted.

Calenick. (© Tony Atkin)

28 JANUARY 1861

Two Italian seamen from the Austrian brig *Guisto P*, Antonio Bonich (24) and Giovanni Rossi (27), went ashore at St Just creek to fill up their water casks. After they had done so, they went into the fields to collect some turnips and herbs. Mistaking hemlock plants for edible herbs, they picked and sampled some with apparent relish. As the tide was out they were unable to leave the beach, so they joined another sailor in looking for oysters. On returning Rossi fell down and started howling with pain, as did Bonich about ten minutes later. Neither still had the power of speech, and they were both perspiring heavily, foaming at the mouths. Within a quarter of an hour they were unconscious, and soon afterwards they were dead.

29 JANUARY 1896

Stephen Smith, a fruiterer who had premises in Arwenack Street, Falmouth, tried to kill himself. His wife Annie, who was many years younger than him, had seen him on the morning of 27 January when they went to visit his daughter at her house at Devonport.

The next day she had a telegram from the daughter, begging her to return at once. When she arrived she found her husband almost senseless after having fallen and cut his head and shoulders. On this day she accompanied him to the station, and he was weeping, 'You see me now, but in a little while you won't see me.' She offered to travel on the train with him, but he told her he would much rather go alone. After the train left she found he had gone to Truro. While he was on his way to Falmouth, he was noticed with an open penknife in his hand, which she assumed he was going to use to cut his tobacco.

When he came home again, his wife refused to let him go out. When she said he could go into the next room, he came back almost at once with a razor in his pocket. Annie and her daughter both ran downstairs as they feared he might be about to harm them. At her request her stepson came to see his father. Later she saw her husband with his throat bandaged.

Although Smith had often suffered from depression and taken to drink, he had never tried to commit suicide before and there had never been any angry words between Smith and his wife. Dr Harris found three incised wounds in his throat; one needed to be stitched, but the other two were superficial. Smith had been drunk at the time.

When he appeared before the magistrates at Falmouth his wife promised to take good care of him, and he said he would sign the pledge. 'I was fourteen years a teetotaller,' he told the Bench, 'and I will guarantee that I'll be a teetotaller again for fourteen years. You will never get me here through drink again.'

30 JANUARY 1867

A double tragedy from Tintagel was reported in the papers. Mr Smith, a donkey proprietor, who was described as 'a strong, middle-aged man' and popular with visitors in the area, had been showing signs of depression for some weeks. Neighbours had heard him threaten suicide, and kept a careful watch on his movements.

On the night of Friday 23 January, Thomas Baker was 'on watch', and accompanied Smith for a walk. When they reached a point at the road open to the sea, Smith suddenly grasped his companion, and a fierce struggle ensued. Smith proved the stronger of the two, and pushed Baker into the water, watched by two helpless women spectators. Once they were in the sea the struggle continued, Baker being held down below the surface until

Tintagel.

Godrevy Lighthouse.
(© Brian, www.geograph.org.uk)

a heavy breaker came in and washed them both away. The body of Smith was washed ashore on Saturday, but that of Baker was not seen again.

31 JANUARY 1938

The steamer *Alba*, a 2,310-ton vessel registered in Panama, struck the rocks at the back of the St Ives headland within 200yds of the shore during a gale. Three men, all from Hungary, were drowned, and the St Ives lifeboat capsized as it returned with survivors from the stricken vessel. Fortunately it righted itself, and many men scrambled back on board, while others, wearing lifejackets, swam to the beach. Hundreds of men and women came down towards the rocks to help, a rocket apparatus crew formed a lifeline, and several men were pulled ashore.

At the inquest on 2 February, complaints were made about the lack of power of the light at Godrevy Lighthouse since its changeover to an unmanned light. One of the officers from the steamer took bearings from it, but on putting back to St Ives the lights from the shore off Porthmear gave them the impression that they were in St Ives Bay.

FEBRUARY

Kynance Cove, visited by the Ibotson family on 10 February 1864, shortly before a member drowned herself at Penzance. (© Dr Neil Clifton)

1 FEBRUARY 1889

A fire broke out in the house of Mr Ball, a rope manufacturer, at Pydar Street, Truro, shortly before midnight, and the fire brigade was called. Mr Ball and his family were in the rooms at the back of the house when the fire started at the front of the building and were able to escape. The house of his neighbour, Julian Butcher, was also set alight and Mr Butcher, his wife, child, his sister-in-law Miss Dennis, and a servant, were at the third-storey windows at the back shouting for help. A policeman on duty fetched a ladder and placed it against the wall, but found it was about 6ft too short to reach the window. Mr Butcher handed his child to the policeman, who had climbed to the top of the ladder, and took it safely to the ground, then climbed up again to rescue Mrs Butcher, who was being suspended from the window by her husband. After this Mr Butcher was helped out, but as he came down the ladder he said that Miss Dennis was still in the burning house. He had heard her drop on the floor, thought she must be overcome by the smoke, and feared she might have suffocated. To his relief she appeared at the window almost immediately, and she was also helped out. Meanwhile the servant had jumped out of another window, falling about 20ft, and was rescued by one of the people who had come to see the fire and be of assistance if needed.

The fire was not completely put out for some hours and the roofs of both houses fell in. Nevertheless, it had been a fortunate escape for everyone concerned, with only one victim. Miss Catherine Symons, who lived in an adjoining house, 'was so excited that she was seized with illness and died.'

2 FEBRUARY 1649

Only three days after King Charles I was executed at Whitehall on 30 January, there was a further blow for the house of Stuart. The *Garland*, a ship carrying the wardrobe belonging to Charles, Prince of Wales (later King Charles II), was wrecked during a great storm. It had been driven from its anchors off St Ives onto the reef, and it took two or three days for boats to rescue the survivors – a man, a boy and a wolfhound. About sixty others on board had perished. Some of the valuables, including a scarlet coat with gold buttons, a coverlet, and several pieces of drapery and other linen, were later washed ashore around Godrevy.

3 FEBRUARY 1830

At about 9 a.m. an engine boiler at United Hills Mine, in the parish of St Agnes, exploded. Nine men, a boy and a girl, who were in the boiler house, and one man, who was in the engine house, were killed. Another nine were seriously injured by a combination of scalding water, stones and bricks, and died within a few hours, and the other three were in such a hopeless state that they were not expected to survive for long.

At an inquest held the next day, Jane Goyne, a dresser of ore at the mine, said she had gone into the boiler house at about 8 a.m. to keep warm. A few minutes later James Sampson, the engine man, asked her to go for a pitcher of water. Only moments after that she heard a tremendous noise, and looking back, saw the steam ascending to a great height, accompanied by a loud rushing noise.

The boiler had undergone a complete overhaul at Redruth Hammer Mill, and had only been in use again for two or three days. It had burst in the bottom part of the tube, one of the strongest parts of the apparatus. It had been the duty of the engine man to regulate the feed of steam, and he had done so not long before the explosion. Nobody was held to blame, and a verdict of accidental death was returned.

4 FEBRUARY 1931

Leading Aircraftman L.C. Oates (56), of St James Street, Penzance, was one of nine men killed in an air disaster at Plymouth. A Blackburn Iris flying boat from RAF Mount Batten with a crew of twelve, travelling at about 70mph, was returning from exercises when it nosedived into Plymouth Sound. According to witnesses, a fountain of water shot up into the air on impact, and it was followed by a shattering explosion. The craft lurched, toppled over on its side and sank with eight men trapped in the hull. At the time the weather and visibility were good, and there was very little wind. Oates, a fitter by trade, had joined the RAF in 1922, and was due to be married in the summer. He had been a keen footballer since his schooldays and played several times for Cornwall.

5 FEBRUARY 1946

Richard Martin (24), a Camborne labourer, pleaded guilty at Bodmin Assizes to causing grievous bodily harm to Miss Edith Webb after she had left the Camborne Regal Cinema on 22 December last. Mr Justice Wriothesley said the fact that the accused had been on bail was, 'the most astounding thing I think I have ever heard,' in view of the seriousness of his crime, and it was most fortunate that no more young women had been attacked. 'I see murder in the offing here as clear as anything,' he said. The police had twice opposed bail being granted. Martin had a previous conviction for stabbing a young woman, whom he had since married, with a penknife. He was sentenced to nine months' imprisonment. The case was referred back to Winchester Assizes to enable medical reports to be put before the judge.

6 FEBRUARY 1839

Jesse Lean, a miner and farmer at Trevarth, had gone to work in the mines when he was summoned home with an urgent message from a fellow worker to say that his wife was unwell. He arrived back to find her soaked in blood with severe head injuries. She was still conscious and told him that a man in a brown coat had forced his way into her bedroom and 'clopped' her over the head. A doctor came to clean and bandage her wounds, but she died that night.

The post-mortem revealed that she had been stabbed three times in the face and once in the ear, and her death was as a result of ruptured blood vessels in the brain arising from the stab wounds.

Nothing had been stolen from the house, and robbery was therefore ruled out as a motive. Jesse and Loveday were known to have quarrelled on occasion and he was initially the main suspect, but several witnesses confirmed that he had been nowhere near the farm when the attack took place. At the inquest some people said they had seen a man prowling outside and running along the lane that morning. After a reward was offered by the parish for the conviction of the murderer, Mr Cock made a full confession and was arrested, but he then retracted it and was released without charge. Police turned their attention again to Jesse Lean, but found insufficient evidence to charge him, and the case remained unsolved.

7 FEBRUARY 1931

Mary Ann Dunhill (79) was found dead, having been bound hand and foot and gagged, on the floor at Pentowan Hotel, Summerleaze Crescent, Bude, where she had helped with housekeeping. The proprietors, Mr and Mrs Crisp, discovered her body when they returned in the evening after being away all day on family business. They then went to look for their chef and handyman Joseph Cowley (29), who had been left in charge all day during their absence; he had absconded and made his way on foot and then by bus to Plymouth. Lily Neilson, his girlfriend who worked at a hotel in Plymouth, was contacted by the police about Mrs Dunhill's death, and knew that it was being treated as murder. She suspected the worst, and asked him why he had run away. When he said he 'got scared,' she made him turn himself in, saying that it was not fair on her 'with all these policemen after me'.

After the police had cautioned him and taken him away for questioning, Cowley confessed that he had robbed the Crisps' rooms in their absence, then started going through the possessions in Mrs Dunhill's room. She caught him red-handed, so in order to stop her from informing on him he seized her by the throat, gagged her and tied her up. He then ran away leaving her, aware that she was still alive.

St Agnes.

When put on trial at Bodmin Assizes on 24 June, charged with murder, he claimed he was too fond of her to want to do her any harm. He told the court that he did not think she would die before Mr and Mrs Crisp returned that evening and found her, and had assumed that they would be able to untie her and she would be none the worse for her ordeal. After retiring for fifteen minutes, the jury convicted him of manslaughter and he was sentenced to seven years' imprisonment.

8 FEBRUARY 1802

Henry Harris James (20), a student from St Agnes, was found dead at his apartments in Jesus College, Cambridge, having previously been in good health. A post-mortem revealed the cause of death to be a burst blood vessel.

9 FEBRUARY 1897

Twelve men working on the reconstruction of the Coldrenick viaduct were killed in an accident when a platform collapsed. An inquest was held into their deaths at Liskeard on 12 February, and Henry Blewett, the foreman, and Samuel Pearse, the ganger, were charged with manslaughter and were granted bail. Blewett told the inquest that he had been working at the same platform earlier that morning and that he would certainly not have done so had he considered it unsafe.

10 FEBRUARY 1864

A case of suicide at Penzance was reported. Six days previously a group consisting of Mr and Mrs Ibotson from Middlesex, his cousin Louisa (34), and a female servant, arrived in the town after staying at Torquay, visited Mitchell's Western Hotel, and took rooms at The Baths. Louisa had

The Promenade, Penzance.

been in robust health until about a year earlier, when she 'adopted deep religious views, and her mind weakened so much that her physician saw cause to advise change of residence and a careful watch on her movements.'

After coming to stay at Penzance the party visited the Lizard and Kynance Cove. On their return to The Baths, just as tea was ready, Louisa rose from her chair in the sitting room and asked them if they would excuse her for a moment. Having a grim foreboding, her cousin asked a servant to go and keep watch on her. He was too late, for about a minute later an alarm was raised on the Promenade that a woman was in the water. She had deliberately thrown herself in.

It was a dark evening and the surf was strong. Coastguards and others tried to come to the rescue, but it was to no avail. Her body had been swept 200–300ft away and was not recovered for three quarters of an hour. By that time, 'it was unbruised, but life was quite extinct'.

11 FEBRUARY 1941

The body of William Hunter (45), of Portadown, County Armagh, was found floating near Falmouth jetty. At the inquest the next day, no evidence was found to suggest that he had been any the worse for drink. He was known as a man of 'jovial disposition' and there was no reason to suspect he would take his own life.

12 FEBRUARY 1908

It was feared that the Fowey schooner *Silverlands*, owned by Mr G. Hodge of Pentewan, whose brother was the captain, had been run into and sunk off the coast of Teignmouth. The ship, a 93-ton vessel built at Sunderland in 1868, had left on 5 February with a cargo of potter's clay for London. Four or five crew were feared to have perished; the only survivor, the mate, was rescued and returned to Teignmouth earlier in the week. An empty lifeboat belonging to the schooner had also been picked up offshore.

13 FEBRUARY 1915

An inquest was held at Liskeard into the death of John George Hann (28), Whip to the East Cornwall hounds, who had drowned while attempting to cross the River Lynher on 1 January in pursuit of a fox.

William John Carne, a gardener of Landrake, said he was in a field in the valley adjoining the River Lynher, and on looking into the river he caught sight of a large bundle. He found it was the body of a man, and with assistance he took it to Bush Farm.

John Hill of Liskeard was among those who rode to the meet at Pillaton on New Year's Day. He said it was a very wet morning, and the river below Pillaton was in flood. During the hunt Hann saw the fox on the other side of the river, and tried to cross the river at a recognised point. Hill heard him cry for help, and fetched a rope, then saw Hann clinging desperately to the branch of a tree, while the horse had gone downstream. Hann became exhausted and had to let go, and before further help could be summoned he had disappeared. At the time the river was about 60yds wide.

14 FEBRUARY 1900

William John Maddern (7), the son of Edwin Maddern, a fish hawker, was drowned at Gwair's Quay, Newlyn. His body was found floating in the seaweed by fishermen in Newlyn harbour and the coroner's jury assumed that he had fallen in accidentally.

However, William's 12-year-old sister, Fanny, later claimed that she had been ordered by her stepmother, Mary, to push him in. Fanny said that Mary had threatened that if she failed to complete the task she would not only deal with William but kill Fanny as well. Fanny therefore accompanied William when he went to try and catch some fish with his piece of string and bent pin. Once he was sitting at the quay she put her hand on his shoulder and pushed him over.

Being afraid to tell her father, she originally said at the inquest that she had tried to persuade her brother to come home, but instead he kicked her and said he wanted to go to the beach, and that she never saw him alive again.

Fishermen at Newlyn. Newlyn was the scene of William Maddern's suspicious death on 14 February 1900.

However, in October she went to live with her aunt, Mrs Wallis, at St Paul Churchtown, and told her the full story.

Mrs Wallis went to the police, and in November Mary Maddern was charged at Penzance with having abetted, counselled and procured Fanny Maddern to commit the murder. The case came to court at Bodmin Assizes before Mr Justice Ridley on 10 November. He asked what evidence was there to corroborate the story, as no depositions had been taken by the coroner at the time. Not until people began to gossip, he said, was there any suspicion that it might have been murder and not an accident. A further inquiry by the coroner might be ordered by the Attorney-General if he thought fit to do so, but if the grand jury took his (the judge's) view of the matter, they would think there was no case made out or deposition upon which the accused should be tried. Mary Maddern was therefore released.

15 FEBRUARY 1905

Frederick Jacobs of Bugle was charged with wounding Nicholas Kent, a clay labourer from Ruddlemore. Late on the evening of 11 February they had been part of a group at General Wolfe Inn, Bodmin Road, and a dispute arose regarding change for drinks. Kent met Jacobs at the back door, and angry words and blows soon followed. Jacobs drew a penknife from his pocket and stabbed Kent in the thigh. The wound would probably have been fatal if the knife had gone any deeper. The accused was committed for trial.

16 FEBRUARY 1904

Just before leaving work at the Lanivet tin mine, Mr Quintrell had blasted a hole charged with dynamite, and he and his comrade, Mr Geak, climbed up the side of the pit to see how much the earth had been loosened. The ground gave way and knocked Quintrell over, and he rolled down to the bottom amid the debris. Geak went to fetch assistance, and others came to the scene with a stretcher, to take him to his home a mile away. A doctor was summoned, but could do nothing to help as Quintrell was already dead. It was the first fatal accident at the mine for more than twenty years.

17 FEBRUARY 1863

Harriet King was charged at Truro Magistrates' Court with assaulting Elizabeth Wellington, who had called King's mother a witch and said she had 'ill-used' a person. When King's previously healthy cat suddenly died, a furious King was convinced it was Wellington's fault and verbally abused then struck her. She was fined 1s and 19s costs.

18 FEBRUARY 1868

The 77-ton ship *Quatre Soeurs* foundered under Gurnard's Head during a west-north-west gale. The coastguard was alerted, but no members of the crew were found, and the vessel soon broke up in the heavy seas and strong wind. Some papers were washed ashore, including various Custom House notes and bills for provisions. Records revealed that she had left Cherbourg on 20 January for Cardiff with a cargo of corn, and the appearance of damage suggested she had been in a collision elsewhere prior to shipwreck. There appeared to be no survivors.

19 FEBRUARY 1928

The battered and bleeding body of Richard Roadley (84), a retired farmer and recluse, was discovered in his cottage at Titson, near Marhamchurch. He was lying on the floor tightly wrapped in a blanket, with a severe head wound. A doctor was summoned immediately, and confirmed that the injury had not been caused by a fall, but that Roadley had been struck with a blunt object. He died from his injuries later that evening, and the police immediately contacted Scotland Yard to help find his attacker.

Roadley had long had a reputation as an elderly eccentric who lived in squalor while apparently sitting on a fortune, having become Lord of the Manor at Scotter, Gainsborough, Lincolnshire, on the death of his brother the previous year. The house had been ransacked, and the contents of the drawers were thrown around the floor.

The village of Marhamchurch.

After four men had been taken in for questioning and released, a trail led the police to William Maynard (36), a rabbit trapper who lived at Poundstock. He was initially unable to account satisfactorily for his movements on the day of the attack, but then admitted to having taken part in a robbery at the cottage, and tried to implicate an associate, Thomas Harris. The latter was detained for questioning for twenty-four hours, but could prove that he had been several miles away at the time of the fatal events that day, and Maynard was charged with murder. He went on trial at Bodmin on 4 June, pleading not guilty. Though the defence tried to suggest that Roadley had died after a fall, Maynard was found guilty. An appeal failed and he was executed at Exeter on 27 July.

20 FEBRUARY 1832

The Brixham schooner *Ebenezer*, sailing from Newport for Topsham with coal, was driven into Portreath during a fierce north-north-west gale. One man was swept away, and the rest of the crew had to cling to the rigging until low tide. Captain Watchem was confined to his bunk with a broken leg, and had no idea of the danger they were in until the vessel struck the rocks, whereupon he sprang up, and broke his leg a second time.

21 FEBRUARY 1952

Bertha Mary Scorse (20), of Newlyn, was sentenced to death for murder. At the opening of her trial at Exeter before Mr Justice Pilcher on 20 February she had pleaded not guilty to murdering her lover Joyce Mary Dunstan (26) of Pool, Camborne. The women had met about two years previously at a sanatorium while they were suffering from tuberculosis, and 'formed a perverted passion' for each other. After being discharged, Dunstan returned briefly to live with her husband, then went to live with Scorse at the latter's mother's home for about sixteen months. During this time there were frequent arguments, perhaps exacerbated by the fact that Dunstan's condition was improving while that of Scorse was deteriorating.

On 12 January 1952 they had a quarrel, and two days later Dunstan walked out. Scorse, along with her sister and an aunt, took a taxi and followed Dunstan to Pool, about fifteen miles away. Scorse claimed that she intended to try and persuade her lover to come back, but when Dunstan came outside to talk to them Scorse stabbed her to death with a dagger. Scorse then ordered the driver to get them away before the police arrived, but he rightly refused. Just before she died, Dunstan made a statement that Scorse had purchased the dagger at the start of their relationship, and said she would not hesitate to use it if anybody ever tried to separate them.

The still gravely ill Scorse was carried into court on a stretcher. John Maude, for the defence, said she knew she was dying, and 'was so frantic in her illness, both mental and physical' that she had no idea what she was doing; 'she was beside herself through disease of the mind.'

On the second day of the trial Dr Matheson, principal medical officer of Brixton Prison, argued for the prosecution that Scorse had refused to be interviewed by him while in Exeter Prison, declared her mental condition was sane, and that her having taken the knife with her when going to see Dunstan on the fatal day was evidence of premeditation. While awaiting trial she had made two suicide attempts by cutting her wrists, and was watched day and night. The jury took an hour to find her guilty, and as sentence of death was passed, Scorse's stretcher was raised in the dock so she could face the judge as he spoke. On 25 February the Home Secretary granted her a reprieve.

22 FEBRUARY 1879

County Magistrates at Truro sent a labourer, Charles Wood, to prison for a month for stealing from a collection of animal bones which were the property of a Mr Teague. They also fined Thomas Phillips 50s for carrying a gun without a licence.

23 FEBRUARY 1817

At about midnight, a row of houses occupied by the poor of the parish of St Buryan, about six miles from Penzance, was discovered to be on fire. The flames spread so rapidly that all the buildings were reduced to ruins in very little time. There were about twenty-seven people living there at the time of the accident, and twenty-one of these managed to save themselves by jumping out of the windows. However, two men and four women were unable to escape, and died.

Perhaps the saddest victim of the inferno was a girl of 19, who suffered from fits and occasional derangement, and had recently been removed to the poorhouse, as the overseers thought 2s a week was too much for her maintenance. Her father was a fisherman, and her mother was blind. The girl had become violent on being separated from her friends, and had to be secured by a chain. She was last seen frantically struggling in the flames, but perished as she could not free herself from the fetters.

24 FEBRUARY 1953

Miles Giffard (26) was hanged at Horfield Prison, Bristol, for the murder of his parents at the family home at Porthpean, overlooking St Austell Bay, on 7 November 1952. He had had a very bad relationship with his father Charles, senior partner in a firm of solicitors, and was unable or unwilling to hold down a job for any length of time. Though his father wanted him to become a solicitor, he dreamed of trying to carve out a career as a professional sportsman. Though he lived at home most of the time, he had visited London from time to time and formed a close relationship with 19-year-old Gabrielle Vallance. His father ordered him to break off the romance and return home, and threatened to cut him off without the proverbial penny if he did not comply. In doing this the solicitor signed his own death warrant, for Miles decided his father would have to die.

After lying in wait for Charles on his return home from work on the evening of 7 November 1952, Miles battered him unconscious with an iron pipe. When his mother, Elizabeth, came home, he attacked her as well. He then transported them, one at a time, in a wheelbarrow to the edge of a cliff and tipped them over.

Their bodies were discovered the next morning after the housemaid found the house empty and had sent her fiancé to report their disappearance to the police. Giffard drove back to London overnight to rejoin Gabrielle and pawn his mother's jewels (something he had previously done at least once before when needing instant funds), but was arrested the following evening and confessed to the murders, saying he must have had a brainstorm.

During his three-day trial at Bodmin, from 4 to 6 February 1953, several witnesses testified to his having received psychiatric help as a child, and the serious doubts as to his mental stability. At the age of two he had been in the care of a nanny who regularly beat him and locked him in a dark room

The footpath leading to Porthpean, along which Miles Giffard pushed his parents' bodies in a wheelbarrow. (© Devon & Cornwall Constabulary)

Charles Giffard's car, photographed by police shortly after he and his wife were murdered. (© Devon & Cornwall Constabulary)

as a punishment, until she was dismissed for cruelty. Nevertheless, in his summing up the judge, Mr Justice Oliver, said Gifford was either bad or mad, guilty or guilty but insane. After retiring for thirty minutes the jury found him guilty, and despite an appeal against the sentence, he went to the gallows.

25 FEBRUARY 1862

Jane Husband (17) arrived late for work at South Caradon Mine. To avoid being seen by the supervisors, she went into the jigging house instead of the tool house as she normally did. Her dress became caught in the jigging machine, and she was crushed to death. At a post-mortem it was established that, surprisingly, not a single bone in her body was broken.

26 FEBRUARY 1869

A carriage was entering Helston by the south road when the horse took fright. A solicitor, Mr Plomer, his daughter and a companion, were in the carriage. After running half a mile, the horse skidded while turning a corner and fell, and the vehicle overturned. Mr Plomer and his fellow passengers were only left with minor injuries, but Henry Perry, the driver, was taken home unconscious with a fractured skull. The carriage was smashed but the horse was uninjured, and Perry later made a good recovery.

Helston.

27 FEBRUARY 1818

Three ships, laden with provisions from Ireland, had recently been wrecked at St Minver, near Padstow, and the shore was visited by several people foraging what they could from the cargo which remained. On this day, two men who ventured too far into the sea in trying to help themselves to some bacon, were overwhelmed by the waves and drowned. Both were married, and left seven children between them. A few days later, another man paid with his life in similar circumstances.

28 FEBRUARY 1839

A woman called on Mr Nott, the relieving officer of St Austell, and asked him to come at once to Watering. She had just found a very ill woman lying in the road, and thought she might have recently given birth to a child. He called some men from the workhouse to go out in a cart and see if there was anything they could do. He and the surgeon went separately to the spot, but they could do nothing to save her life. They found out that she was a Mrs Bell, and went to look for her husband, as there was every possibility that he might have caused her death, either deliberately or through negligence.

Working on descriptions from those who knew Mr Bell, the receiving officer and a police constable searched all the beer shops and lodging houses in the district to try and find him. He was described as a travelling tinker, about 5ft 5in tall, rather stout, with a dark complexion, and was last seen wearing corduroy breeches and leggings, high shoes, a new black hat, and a green plush waistcoat with sleeves, but no coat.

Several witnesses came forward to testify that they had seen him knock down his wife, kick and beat her for being drunk, and then leave her. She tried to walk to St Austell, but collapsed and bled to death. As she was so intoxicated, only one person had stopped to try and help her. Nothing was found to substantiate the belief that she was pregnant or had given birth. On

St Austell.

being apprehended her husband would have faced a charge of manslaughter, but he eluded capture. He was never seen again, and the couple's two young children were abandoned in a lodging house near St Austell.

29 FEBRUARY 1944

John Richards (62), a well-known agriculturalist of St Martin-in-Meneage, near Helston, was riding on the shaft of a horse-drawn cart laden with straw. As he was approaching his farm the horse took fright, he was thrown from the seat, and the wheels passed over him. He was unconscious when found and rushed to hospital but died shortly afterwards, leaving a widow but no children.

MARCH

North Hill, near Wadebridge, where Nevell Norway's body was discovered. On 20 March 1844 William and James Lightfoot went on trial, charged with his murder. (By kind permission of West Briton)

1 MARCH 1905

Two men lost their lives in Falmouth harbour. At about 7 p.m. a ship's boat left the quay to proceed to the Norwegian barque *Ragna*, from Melbourne, which was in the harbour. Aboard were Captain Bache and two seamen, one of whom was named Ellis Jannson. The boat was caught by a squall, the ballast shifted, and it capsized. The captain could not swim, and clung to the bottom of the boat, but the other two men swam for the shore on an oar. Jannson told his mate he was getting exhausted and the latter relinquished the oar to him, struck out, and reached the shore in safety. Jansson sank before he could reach land. The boat was later discovered, but by then Bache had also drowned.

2 MARCH 1855

An inquest was held at Redruth on Henry Turner (17), a miner who worked at Wheal Buller. On the evidence of James Thomas, under whom he worked, Turner got on a ladder to go down to his work with a lighted rope in one hand, which he intended to use to light a candle at the bottom. While Thomas was watching and waiting for him to go down a few staves before he got onto the ladder himself, he saw some sparks fall from the rope onto the hand which Turner was using to hold the ladder. He immediately let go and fell. His body was found between the twenty and thirty fathoms level in the mine, suspended by the cuff of his coat to a nail projecting from the dividings of the shaft. He had received several injuries in the fall, particularly about the head, and died later that week.

3 MARCH 1904

At Penzance and some of the neighbouring villages, an earthquake was felt at around 1 p.m. There was a distinct trembling noise, and many people declared that they felt the shock concurrent with the report, which was at first thought to be an explosion. Nobody was injured and no damage to property was reported.

4 MARCH 1784

The body of Ann Cargill (24), actress and opera singer, was recovered from the wreck of the *Nancy* which was dashed to pieces off the Scilly Isles about a week earlier. It had sunk off the uninhabited island of Rosevear. Contemporary newspaper accounts described her as 'floating in her shift' with an infant child at her bosom.

Cargill had made her debut on the stage at the age of 11 at Covent Garden, taking lead roles, although she was under the legal age. Her angry father won a court order confining her to his house, but she defied him, and in 1776 she was cast in the lead role of Polly in John Gay's *The Beggar's Opera*. Her father tried to seize her one night on her way to the theatre, but he was restrained by the audience and the performance went ahead.

In 1780 she was said to be the world's highest-paid actress, but her affairs and elopement shocked London society. Her lover, Captain John Haldane, said to be the unluckiest commander in the British East India Co. as he had already lost one ship, was stationed in Calcutta so she went to join him. The Prime Minister, William Pitt, said in Parliament that 'an actress should not be defiling the pure shores of India', and recalled her home. They were on their way home when the *Nancy* was lost, with thirty-six crew and about twelve passengers drowned.

It was said that Cargill was carrying jewels and cash worth about £200,000 with her, but none of them were ever found. She was buried at Rosevear Island, but her body was later disinterred and reburied at Old Town Church, St Mary's. It is said that the ghosts of her and her child still haunt Rosevear to this day.

In September 2008 it was revealed that two divers, both local historians, had found a cannon and other artefacts from a wreck dating from the correct period nearly half a mile from where the *Nancy* supposedly went down. They believed that the vessel had sunk on Western Rocks, and that the ship's passengers and crew had taken to a smaller boat which capsized as they were trying to land.

5 MARCH 1940

An inquest was held at Saltash into the death of William Henry Welsh of Carkeel and was presided over by Colonel Toogood, the deputy coroner. Dr Hugh Robinson said he had received a message at 6.15 a.m. and went to Fore Street, Saltash, where he found the deceased lying in the road. He was unconscious, bleeding from the nose, mouth and right ear. He was taken to hospital, but died at 1.30 p.m. Death was due to a fracture at the base of the skull. The doctor said that the deceased was found lying by his cycle, and drew the conclusion that Welsh had been thrown over the handlebars. Colonel Toogood warned that people should exercise the utmost caution during the blackout.

6 MARCH 1919

At a meeting of West Penwith Rural District Council at Penzance, Dr Richmond reported on a recent outbreak of anthrax at Mill Pool, St Austell. The Board of Agriculture had declared it an infected area, and two bullocks had had to be destroyed.

Penzance.

7 MARCH 1962

Gales and high tides battered Penzance, Newlyn and other nearby Cornish resorts during the night. When high tide ebbed at Penzance on the morning of 8 March, local people ventured to the seafront to see what damage the gale had caused. According to reports received by the British Insurance Association, the initial estimates of the damage to private property in Penzance and Newlyn amounted to £100,000, and adjusters were sent to the area later that same day to help hundreds of householders with their claims. The Mayor of Penzance, Richard Matthews, opened a disaster fund, which in the first few hours reached more than 300 guineas, and the deputy town clerk, Mr J.H.D. Nicholas, said there was no doubt that the town would need government help. There was considerable distress among residents living in the Penzance and Newlyn areas, with between 200 and 300 houses affected.

8 MARCH 1927

Leslie Knight, of King Street, Torpoint, was fined £1 for jumping off the Torpoint ferry while it was in motion. On behalf of Cornwall County Council, Elliott Square said that there was a growing practice among work-men, especially dockyard employees, of opening the gates, walking to the ends of the prows, and jumping off before the vessel was stationary. It might seem a minor offence, but steps had to be taken for the protection of the public, and to let them know that there were regulations forbidding them to leave the ferry before the prows had been lowered and the

The Torpoint ferry.

gates officially opened. There had been two recent cases when small groups of men had taken charge of the prows, and the captain had been forced to stop the vessel. On one occasion they had been lucky to avert a serious accident, when a woman fell in the act of jumping ashore and the prows passed over her body.

9 MARCH 1896

While work was being carried out in a field on a farm occupied by Mr Markham, at St Martin's, near Helston, adjoining St Martin's churchyard, a labourer found the coffin of a child just below the surface of the ground. A breastplate on it identified it as the remains of the infant child of John Pascoe, who formerly farmed in the neighbourhood, but had since acquired a farm in Oxfordshire. The child had been buried about thirteen years earlier. The pick which the labourer used pierced the lid of the coffin, which was rotten and fell to pieces. It was thought that while digging a new grave in the churchyard, the coffin might have proved an obstacle and been removed into the field, but the sexton denied all knowledge of any such thing. The affair caused some distress to the child's immediate relations. Mr Markham said that the coffin must have been placed in the field since 1893, as he ploughed the field that year and was sure he would have discovered it if it had been there at the time.

10 MARCH: Redruth

The name Redruth is said to be derived from the colour of St Ruth's cloak, and for several centuries a legend persisted that that no child who had been baptised with the water from St Ruth's Well would ever be hanged. This is disputed by those who say there are other, more likely stories about the origin of the name, the most popular being that it is named after the river which runs red from the minerals mined locally. Another suggests that it comes from the Cornish name, Rhyd-ruth; Rhyd an older form of *Res*, a Cornish equivalent to a ford (across a river) and *ruth*, meaning red.

In 1869 it was estimated that Redruth had more prostitutes than anywhere in Cornwall, due mainly to a rise in the town's population of over 11,000 due to mining activity. Women who had lost their husbands

Redruth mine, c. 1890.

in accidents down the mines had little, if any, choice other than 'the oldest profession' or the workhouse.

11 MARCH 1865

Richard Burrows of Creegbrawse attacked Elizabeth Evans, of Bissoe Pool, and was charged at West Powder Petty Sessions in April for assaulting her. She said that he entered her house, caught her by the throat, and brandished a stick over her head, threatening to kill her. In his defence he told the court that he was convinced she was a witch. 'I think she ill-wished me, and I pretended to give her a scratch. I have heard that if you go and bring blood they can never hurt you any more. I was not well in body and mind; and she pretends to do witchcraft, and takes money.' He was fined 1s and costs.

12 MARCH 1941

Alfred Cook, a butcher of Arch House, East Looe, was fined £15 at Liskeard for receiving stolen oats. Charles Welsh and Francis Phillips, both of Morval, pleaded guilty to theft. They were bound over for two years, and each was ordered to pay 12s 6d costs. Both men were farm labourers employed at Morval Barton by Mr Carsons, who had reported several bags missing and informed the police. When questioned, Welsh and Phillips admitted that they had stolen them. Cook pleaded not guilty, saying he had no idea the oats were stolen property. However, he admitted that he had only paid 10s a bag, as opposed to the normal merchant's price of 15s and that he knew the men were farm labourers and did not grow oats themselves. Though the bags were generally delivered at night, he claimed that he did not think there was anything suspicious about this.

13 MARCH 1956

Michael Woodfall (34), former managing director of the Royal Talbot Hotel, Lostwithiel, was charged at the Old Bailey with theft. The prosecuting counsel said that he had been released from gaol in July 1955 after serving seven years

GENERAL VIEW OF EAST RIVER TO EAST LOOE

East Looe.

for stealing French francs. Only four months later, his relations had helped him to obtain the post at the hotel. Here he entertained Mr Williams, a jeweller, who had brought some samples of items for inspection and sale. Woodfall had studied them and a sum of over £6,000 was mentioned. The next day Woodfall, Williams, an assistant, and Helen Heckman went to London together. 'Miss Heckman' was Woodfall's secretary, and also his fiancée – or so he believed. In the evening he donned the uniform of a Major, something to which he was not entitled, and took Williams and a few other friends out to the Ritz and various clubs. At the weekend Woodfall gave Williams a cheque for £6,000, drawn on the hotel account, for the jewellery he had chosen, and asked if the diamond and ruby clip could be handed over to him immediately for Miss Hickman to wear.

Early next week Williams returned to the hotel, but Woodfall and the clip had gone, and nobody knew where. In January he was traced to Ireland, where he had pledged the clip in another name in Dublin. He pleaded guilty, saying that he committed the theft 'under an irresistible impulse', and needed medical treatment, not punishment. Detective Sergeant Burt told the court that Woodfall had a string of previous convictions dating back to 1939.

For the defence, Christmas Humphreys said that Woodfall was a psychopath suffering from emotional instability and insecurity. He had committed the offences during a period of 'balloon-like emotional mentality, his mind blown up with fantasies of all kinds.' Woodfall claimed he had ordered jewellery to the value of £6,000 for Miss Heckman and did a great deal of showing off to impress her, but then she admitted that she was already married to someone else, and he panicked. He did not know what he was doing until the day he was arrested, and then, realising there was nothing ahead for him but 'a long term of intolerable imprisonment', attempted suicide. Woodfall begged to be given a chance, as he had been sent to prison time after time, 'and it has done nothing', but was sentenced to nine years' 'preventive detention'.

14 MARCH 1895

William Henry Webb was charged by Penryn magistrates with stealing two fowls at Carharrack on 5 March. William Davey told the Bench that he had thirty-three or thirty-four fowls in his poultry house on the previous night. Next morning he found a fowl's head, feathers and blood spattered about outside and found that two of his birds had gone. At Webb's house he saw two birds and he identified one of them as one of those missing, as well as seeing feathers resembling that of the other missing bird. The head, which was produced in court, seemed to have been torn from the body of the fowl. Davey spoke of visiting Webb the day after the theft. On taking his boots off, he saw that Webb's left boot had dung and feathers sticking to the bottom. Outside he found feathers scattered in the direction of Davey's poultry house, and footmarks corresponded with the accused's boot.

When his wife urged him to tell the truth, Webb said that as he was returning from St Day, he heard one of Davey's fowls cry. Looking over the hedge, he saw a man at the back of the premises, who then ran away and threw the birds down. He did not know the man, but he picked the birds up and took them home. Constable Sleeman gave evidence that the accused said he had been to the St Day election with some friends, but got drunk and therefore could not account for what had happened. Webb pleaded for leniency as he had a wife and five children, and had been a week under remand. He had previously been fined at Camborne for theft. The chairman, Mr Beauchamp, sentenced him to two months' imprisonment with hard labour.

15 MARCH 1922

An inquest was held at Morwenstow on the death of Annie Burrow (22) of Marsland Farm, after her body had been found on Marsland Beach. Her father, Samuel, said his wife and three daughters (including Annie) had dinner together on Sunday 12 March. He had not been aware of Annie having been in any trouble, and she did not seem unhappy or depressed, but was a little more reserved than usual. She was normally quite lively, and he had never heard her make any suggestion of taking her own life. The last time he saw her alive was after dinner. She went out about 2 p.m. and was generally back by 4 p.m. to help with work on the farm. When she had not returned by 6 p.m. he and his wife went to look for her. On their way to the beach road, he saw footprints which he thought were those of his daughter, though there were no other marks. After obtaining assistance from others, he searched for her until 1 a.m., but found nothing. The search resumed at 6 a.m. and three hours later her body was found near Gull Rock. Her father thought she had gone on the beach and been swept away by the tide, but could not swim. A verdict of 'found drowned' was returned in the absence of any evidence to the contrary.

16 MARCH 1871

All hope was given up for the crew of a fishing smack, the *Desire*, which was run down in Mount's Bay earlier in the week by an iron sailing ship, the *Coolie*. The smack went down almost immediately after the collision. In the darkness it was apparently not seen by the *Coolie* until disaster was inevitable. A young man, Mr Strike, managed to scramble up the ship's bows, despite having a broken leg. He was taken by the other vessel to Liverpool, and after his statement about the disaster was telegraphed to Porthleven, there was some excitement among the families of the crew, who all lived there. Nevertheless hopes that some of the others might have been able to save themselves were soon dashed. A fund was opened for the bereaved and destitute widows and children. The smack and fishing gear were said to be of some considerable value.

17 MARCH 1929

Jack Pooley (28), of the Truro Poor Law Institution, was summoned for refractory conduct. The master of the institution, Mr A. Lugg, said Pooley was a source of continual annoyance to the officials and other inmates, and he was compelled to bring him before the court for the maintenance of discipline. Pooley had always been sympathetically treated, but persistently took advantage of the leniency shown towards him. That morning he had attempted to countermand an order given by the porter Mr Williams to another inmate, and then invited the porter to 'come outside the gate'. On the previous Sunday Pooley had taken off his coat and started to fight the gardener. He was sentenced to fourteen days' imprisonment.

18 MARCH 1852

The *Exeter Flying Post* reported that the Revd Walter Gee, rector of Week St Mary, had recently died, 'ten days after receiving from a favourite cat a wound in the arm which resulted in mortification.'

St Mary's Church, Week St Mary. (© Nicola Sly)

19 MARCH 1935

Nellie Goldsworthy, of Falmouth Road, Redruth, was charged at Truro with embezzling £12 15s 6d belonging to her employers, Messrs W.J. Roberts & Son, Truro. She pleaded not guilty and applied for legal aid, saying that her husband was an outfitter and they had their own business but no means. They were financially dependent on her mother-in-law. The Chairman of the Bench said that she faced five other charges of obtaining goods by false pretences.

20 MARCH 1840

Brothers William and James Lightfoot, two notorious highway robbers, went on trial at Bodmin, charged with the murder of Nevell Norway (39), a merchant, on his return home to Wadebridge after market day on 8 February. Norway's horse had returned home riderless with a heavily bloodstained saddle, and a search revealed his body in a ditch about two miles away. He had received several blows to the face and head from a blunt instrument, and died from multiple skull fractures. Two men had been seen loitering at the place where the murder was later committed, and suspicion fell on the Lightfoot brothers, who had a reputation in the area for poaching and housebreaking. After being arrested and escorted to gaol, each tried to blame the other for the man's death. Not long before the court proceedings opened, a labourer gathering sticks near the site of the murder found a stick in the hedgerow, with a large oval knob on one end. Despite recent rainfall, it still bore bloodstains. He took it to the magistrates in Wadebridge, and it was identified as the likely murder weapon.

The brothers pleaded not guilty, but the evidence suggested otherwise, and the jury only took two minutes to deliver their guilty verdict. The brothers

William and James Lightfoot, who were hanged for the murder of Nevell Norway. (By kind permission of West Briton*)*

were convicted and hanged at Bodmin Gaol on 13 April. Norway left a widow and six children, all below the age of nine. His widow Sarah (36) died, apparently from heart disease, only six months after the murder.

21 MARCH 1942

Mrs Annie Harvey (57), of Salt Ponds, Mousehole, was knocked down by a bus and killed. An inquest was held at Penzance on 24 March. A witness saw her walking towards the main road from Pendrea Lane, Chyandour, and as she reached the road she noticed a bus approaching Penzance, and raised her hand to stop it. Instead of giving the driver time to stop, she immediately stepped in front of the bus. The bus driver swerved to the side to avoid an accident, but the front near the lamp struck Mrs Harvey and knocked her down. The coroner was satisfied that the bus had been driven carefully and no blame could be attached to the driver.

Mousehole harbour.

22 MARCH 1961

Severe erosion at Polurrian Cove took the remaining half of Chyvean House, which had begun falling down the 250ft cliff earlier in the week. Half of 'Trenython', the house next door, was also lost to the elements and the cliff was still crumbling away. Villagers were concerned for the state of the road along the cliff top, which led to another eight houses and was now only 30ft from the edge. The nearest of these houses was now only 80ft away, whereas the previous week the distance had been at least 140ft. Meanwhile Kenneth Adams, the owner of Chyvean House, had to move into a caravan home at Mullion village as a temporary measure.

23 MARCH 1864

The Times reported a case concerning the maltreatment of a madman in Cornwall, which had come before the Western Assizes at Bodmin. For eleven years Samuel Porter had kept his brother Robert confined in a single room. There was no fireplace or any other provision for warming the room; the only article of furniture was the frame of a truckle-bed with laths across, and the only ventilation was a sash window. Robert had had but one change of scenery, when his brother moved house about a year earlier and he had been taken to a new room, at dead of night – in a wheelbarrow.

When the Commissioners for Lunacy entered his room they found him behind the door, squatting on his hands, his legs doubled up, his knees against his chest, his heels against his thighs, the feet being crossed one over the other. There was no bedding or clothing in the room, only three pieces of sacking, which he had wrapped round himself to keep warm. The stench was intolerable, and the floor was described as 'a miniature cesspool.' He was fed with ordinary family food served out of a dirty frying pan and with tea from a filthy pewter pot.

In his youth he had been good-looking and intelligent; however, when he was about 25 his mind gave way, and he had been mad for about thirty years. His father had looked after him until he died in 1850, when a sister took over the responsibility. They had both treated him kindly, but the sister went to America in 1853, leaving Robert to the tender mercies of his younger brother. A small weekly sum accruing from property left by his father, about 7s, was paid to Samuel Porter for looking after him.

When Samuel was tried on a charge of neglect the jury returned a verdict of guilty, but said, 'they did not think the defendant was aware of the law, and therefore they recommended him to mercy.' However, in the view of *The Times*, 'no man could commit such disgusting brutality as Samuel Porter without knowing very well that he was violating some law, and that if the law of the land could not by some accident reach him it ought to do so.'

24 MARCH: The Notorious James Thomas

James Thomas, renowned in the contemporary press in the nineteenth century as 'a conjurer from the parish of Illogan', offered to remove a spell from a lady who was the wife of a magistrate. A warrant was issued for his arrest on the grounds that he had proposed to 'commit a most disgraceful offence.' The *West Briton* called him 'a drunken, disgraceful, beastly fellow who ought to be sent to the treadmill.' It continued:

We have purposely withheld the names of a number of Thomas' egregious dupes, with which we are furnished, believing that the badgering which they have doubtless received from their friends has proved a sufficient punishment for them, and that their eyes are now thoroughly opened to the gross and disgraceful imposture that has been practised upon them.

Torpoint.

25 MARCH 1904

An inquest was held at Torpoint on the death of Samuel Ryall, a shipwright pensioner of the town, who was found dead on his bedroom floor. After hearing evidence from Dr S.G. Vinter, the jury returned a verdict of death from natural causes, probably heart disease.

26 MARCH 1892

Mr J.H. Ferris, a Truro solicitor, deputy coroner of Cornwall, member of the City Council, and lieutenant of the Truro Volunteers, killed himself. Since his wife died two months earlier he had been in a very despondent frame of mind. Unable to live without her, he went and lay on her grave, where he shot himself.

27 MARCH 1820

At the Cornwall Assizes, the Grand Jury issued a bill against Lyndon Evelyn and James Graham, who had been returned as MPs for St Ives in the last election; against James Halse, the town clerk, their agent; his relatives and clerk, Richard and William Hitchens; and James Young and Walter Young, for a conspiracy to return the Members at the election by means of bribery and corruption. A petition was being prepared to the House of Commons against the late return, and four eminent Counsel of the Western Circuit were being retained to conduct the prosecutions and petition. After an adjournment, the case came before the Court of King's Bench on 17 December 1821. There had been three candidates, Evelyn, Graham, and Sir Walter Stirling, and when the election was declared in favour of the first two, Stirling petitioned against the return, alleging that the successful candidates were guilty of bribery and corruption. The petition was referred to a Select Committee and the defendant, who had served in South America against Spanish troops, was examined as a witness in support of the allegations of the petition. It was alleged on that occasion that he had falsely deposed that Halse, the agent for the successful candidates, had in his address to the electors collectively, and to some of them individually, 'that they had better make up their minds and vote in favour of Mr Evelyn and Mr Graham, for if not, they would get nothing by the votes they were to give.' The jury dismissed the case.

28 MARCH 1845

Three men, Messrs Colmer, Hocking and Bone, were at work underground in Charlestown United mines, St Austell. While Colmer and Hocking were tamping a hole, or a crack in the rock, the charge went off and ignited some powder in a nearby barrel. Colmer was blown to pieces, and his companions apparently 'were a long time collecting his scattered remains, which were taken up and carried home in a sack.' Hocking was badly wounded in the right side of his head, but Bone escaped injury, as he had gone to get some tamping when the explosion occurred.

Charlestown.

29 MARCH 1940

Arthur Parker, brother of Revd J.L. Parker, vicar of St Julitta Church, Lanteglos, fell to his death from a very high cliff onto the jagged rocks of Polruan. At an inquest early the next week the coroner said Parker ventured further than he should have done, and had an attack of giddiness on top of the cliff and fell over. A stick and cap were lying on the path on the edge. Death was due to multiple fractures of the skull.

30 MARCH 1956

Several hundred young Japanese larch trees were burned in a fire on the Forestry Commission plantation at Driftwood, Glyn Valley, near Bodmin. A group of the commission's fire-fighters were helped by members of the Bodmin unit of Cornwall County Fire Service, and between them succeeded

St Julitta Church, Lanteglos.

in confining the blaze to an area of three acres and extinguished it in a little under an hour. Later that day the Bodmin fire unit put out a gorse fire at Restormel Road, Lostwithiel, caused when a bonfire ignited undergrowth.

31 MARCH 1872

The safety fuse factory of Beckford, Smith & Co. at Camborne was the scene of an unfortunate accident in the morning. About a hundred girls were employed at the factory in six different rooms, each one having a machine driven by steam power for spinning the fuse.

On the evening of 28 March work was suspended for the purpose of cleaning out the boiler, and three girls were ordered to clean up one of the rooms on Saturday morning. They were joined by some of the girls from other departments at the factory. When they had done their work, it was thought that some loose powder in the chinks of the wooden floor became ignited by a spark from a match or something else, and made contact with the fuse near the door. There was no explosion, but the burning of the fuse caused dense smoke, and the girls became frightened. One of them immediately ran out of the room, but the others hesitated, and as they tried to reach the door they were overpowered by the smoke, and fell down together. As the girl who escaped in time did not raise the alarm, the engineer was under the impression that nobody was left in the room. The building was undamaged, but the eight girls were later found in a heap, all clinging together. One or two who had fallen against the fuse were slightly burnt, but the rest looked as if they had merely gone to sleep. At a post-mortem it was found that they had died of suffocation.

APRIL

The passenger train from Plymouth to Penzance, after a derailment at Doublebois
on 13 April 1895.

1 APRIL, 1824

Amy (or Emma) George (19), who lived at Redruth and worked in the local tin mine, went on trial at Launceston on a charge of murdering her brother Benny. She was an impressionable young girl who had been attending Methodist Revival meetings in the town for several weeks. As a result her family found her behaviour increasingly odd; on 1 March she told her mother she thought she was going out of her mind, and a couple of days later she told her mother earnestly that she was tempted to murder her. After this her worried mother took advantage of her absence at the next Revival meeting to hide any knives in the house. Nevertheless the girl had decided she was going to kill somebody, and on 4 March when she saw two boys playing near a mineshaft along the road she was strongly tempted to throw one of them down. That evening she had supper with her younger brother Benny (6), then casually asked him if he would like to go to heaven. 'Yes, when I die,' he replied. She then took a black silk handkerchief from a washing line hanging across the room, tied it round his neck, and used it to hang him from a crook hanging behind the door. She then went next door and told her neighbours with some anguish what she had done. By the time they could reach him, he was dead, and she told them that she was willing to die for her deed. The jury found her not guilty of murder, and the judge ordered her to be retained in custody. This, he assured her family and friends, would only be a temporary measure, and 'she would not be kept long from them.'

2 APRIL, 1821

John Barnicoat (24) and John Thompson (17) were both hanged at Launceston for the murder of William Hancock, a farmer, while he was returning from Helston Market on 12 August 1820. Hancock was accosted by three men, but ignored their orders to stop. Shots rang out; he fell from his horse, and was beaten as he lay on the ground. His assailants went through his pockets but only found 2s. He was left for dead but picked up, still just conscious, and taken to a nearby house. The trio also set upon a labourer and his wife returning from market a little later. They were wounded but soon recovered, and were able to recognise and name Barnicoat, John Thompson and his brother Thomas, who were arrested. Before Hancock died later that week he also identified Barnicoat and John Thompson as the guilty men.

The trial of all three opened on 30 March, but as Thomas had not been named in Hancock's deathbed statement, the case against him was not proven and he was acquitted. The other two went to the scaffold. There are grounds for believing that Barnicoat was innocent, as he claimed, and that another man of the same name, an itinerant farm labourer from Tregony

Helston.

who moved from one farm to another while helping with the harvests, might have been the murderer. It is said that he fled to Australia to escape justice, but was so conscience-stricken that when he died there some years later, he bequeathed his entire estate to the family of his namesake to try and make amends.

3 APRIL 1935

Patrick Hanlon, of Bridge Street, St Blazey, was summoned for causing wilful damage to a street lamp, the property of St Austell Urban Council, and two windows and a door belonging to Mr Sowden, St Blazey. Ethelbert Lee, a chauffeur, also of St Blazey, told the magistrates that while in his house he heard two separate panes of glass being smashed, and was about to go out when the front panel of his door was broken in. As he went into the street, he saw the defendant running away. Constable Hoskin said that three panes of glass in one window and a glass panel were smashed, as well as two panes in the street lamp and a mirror. He picked up some stones that he thought had caused the damage. The defendant said he knew nothing about the incident, and at the time it was supposed to have happened, he was indoors in bed. He was fined £2 10s on each charge, and ordered to pay costs as well as 17s 4d damages, as an alternative to two months' imprisonment.

St Blazey.

4 APRIL, 1945

An inquest was held at Oxford into the death of John Albert Wilkinson (19), a Great Western Railway fireman at Station Road, Fowey. He was on temporary duties at Oxford railway station, where he died from severe head injuries after being knocked down by a passenger train on 24 March. Frederick Prentice, the engineman of the goods train of which Wilkinson had been fireman, said he had got down from his cabin to go to the relief cabin. He was unaware that a train from Sheffield was passing at the same time. Prentice could not find Wilkinson at first, so he searched the line and eventually found his body.

5 APRIL, 1907

Thomas Polmeor (13), who was mentally disabled, appeared before St Ives Magistrates' Court. He was charged with murdering William Davis, a baby aged 4 months, who was found decapitated on the afternoon of 14 March after being left in his care at the family home in Digey Square while the mother was out shopping. Evidence was given that after his arrest the prisoner had made several contradictory statements to the police, among them one in which he said, 'Me put baby in tray of water. Me washed baby's legs. Me cut baby's head off. Baby kicked cradle and cried. Baby teasy old thing. Won't do it any more, policeman.' He also said that he loved the baby dearly, and while looking after him had given him a piece of cake before putting him to sleep in his cradle. Throughout the hearing he laughed repeatedly 'in a half-witted manner'. His father said that he had been taken out of school because the teachers and other pupils found his presence disruptive.

6 APRIL, 1943

Gordon Trenoweth (33) was hanged at Exeter Gaol for the murder of Albert Bateman, a tobacconist, at his shop at Arwenack Street, Falmouth, on Christmas Eve 1942. When Bateman did not return home after close of business his wife went to look for him at the premises. After finding the door locked, she fetched the police. They found him lying on the floor; he had been battered to death.

A revolver was discovered in the shop, and records showed that Trenoweth, a local man who had had a police record since being sentenced for larceny in his youth, had had access to the weapon. When he was arrested on the evening of Christmas Day, among the items found on him was a banknote that was later proved to have been torn and repaired with a letterhead by Bateman at his shop.

The trial opened at Exeter on 11 February and lasted for five days. On the first day, after giving evidence, Mrs Bateman collapsed and had to be carried

The body of Albert Bateman, behind the counter of his shop in Arwenack Street, Falmouth. (© Devon & Cornwall Constabulary)

from the court. Two witnesses confirmed that the unemployed and normally hard-up prisoner had been spending money quite freely at the Market Tavern in Falmouth later on Christmas Eve. The jury found him guilty, but 'with a strong recommendation to mercy', as they considered that the killing had not been premeditated. Nevertheless an appeal was dismissed, and when Thomas Pierrepoint led Trenoweth to the gallows, he became the last man to be hanged at Exeter Gaol.

7 APRIL, 1957

Mr A.E. Cook, of Everton Villas, Launceston, was taken to hospital suffering from facial injuries and shock after a motoring accident. He was driving his car down Windmill Hill towards the town, when it went out of control and crashed into the wall of a butcher's shop.

8 APRIL, 1895

Falmouth magistrates fined William George Brown, mate of the ketch *Jane Milton*, 5s with 2s 6d costs for being drunk and incapable on 6 April. He had been arrested by Constable Warren, who was in court to give evidence. Brown had had two glasses of brandy, and said he did not know what was put into the spirit, but it overcame him. At the same sessions James Murrish and Samuel Clark, who had walked from Penzance to Falmouth, were sentenced to fourteen days' imprisonment for begging.

9 APRIL, 1858

Major Coker and his coachman went on a small boat on his fishpond at Prideaux, near St Blazey, to clear the weeds. They accidentally upset the boat and fell into the water. The coachman could not swim and, although Coker was a good swimmer, he became entangled in the rope attached to the rake they had been using; both men were drowned.

10 APRIL, 1917

A fire broke out in the afternoon at Keveral Barton Farm, a quarter of a mile from Downderry. It had started in a beam left exposed in the chimney, and by the time it was discovered at about 5 p.m., the flames had taken hold. Furniture was moved to safety from the premises, and the Liskeard and Looe fire brigades were telephoned, but the strong wind soon fanned the fire into a blaze and before any assistance could arrive, the farmhouse was gutted.

11 APRIL, 1836

A farmer on the Isles of Scilly lost several of his stock. He thought his misfortunes were due to witchcraft, and consulted one of his neighbours as to the best method of breaking the spell. The advice given him was to burn a calf alive, which he promptly did. Whether it succeeded in its effect was not recorded.

12 APRIL, 1900

Eleven lives were lost after a Lowestoft fishing smack, *Peace and Plenty*, put into Padstow harbour on the evening of 11 April, and anchored in apparent safety. At the time there was a strong westerly gale blowing, accompanied by heavy, breaking seas. Shortly after midnight pilots put off to bring the smack in, but before they reached her the cable parted, and she began to drift across the harbour into a dangerous bay. Lifeboat signals were immediately sounded, and the steam lifeboat and rowing boat were promptly manned. The former put out into the mouth of the harbour, to reach the fishing craft in deep water, but the latter, the *Arab*, took a straight course, and was soon anchored alongside the drifting vessel. Suddenly a huge wave struck the *Arab*, breaking eight oars and throwing eight men into the sea. They were eventually rescued, but it was found impossible to give any assistance to the Lowestoft craft, which quickly drifted ashore. Meanwhile the rocket apparatus was brought into play, and eventually connection between the boat and land was established. Five members of the crew and a boy were

The wrecks of two lifeboats which tried to rescue those on the fishing smack Peace and Plenty *off the coast at Padstow in 1900, during which eleven men were drowned.* (Penny Illustrated Paper and Illustrated Times)

saved, but three others were lost. The *Peace and Plenty* was completely wrecked, though some of her nets were saved. Unfortunately the steam lifeboat crossing the bay was capsized by another large wave, and drifted bottom upwards onto the rocks. Three of her crew were washed ashore, two in a very exhausted condition, but the other eight were drowned.

13 APRIL, 1895

The 5 p.m. passenger train from Plymouth to Penzance, consisting of two engines, five coaches, a meat van and two horse boxes, was wrecked near Doublebois. It had been rounding a curve on an embankment near Clinnick viaduct, travelling at over 40mph, when the leading engine turned inwards, and dragging down the soil, became partially buried. Simultaneously the second engine was flung on its side, at right angles across both lines. The first coach, consisting of the guard's van and three third-class compartments, was swung around with great force broadside against the overturned engine, completely wrecking it. Although the drivers of both engines stuck to their posts and applied the vacuum brake, the train continued, ploughing uphill into a cutting with a steep bank rising high on one side and an equally steep embankment on the other, descending into a valley some 200ft deep. The up and down lines were completely blocked by the derailment, and about thirty people including passengers, drivers, stokers and a guard suffered from shock or were injured, four seriously, though no lives were lost. The driver of the first engine was scalded on the chest, and suffered cuts and bruises, while the driver of the second engine was flung into an adjoining field but only slightly hurt, and the stoker fell between the engine and the first carriage. Doctors from Bodmin and Plymouth were soon on the scene to attend to those injured.

Ten years earlier, a driver had been killed in a similar accident at the same spot. The lines were blocked for the rest of the day but had been cleared by early the next morning.

A report issued by the Railway Department of the Board of Trade in June concluded that in future two engines should not be allowed on any down train between Doublebois and Bodmin Road, as it was unsuitable for very fast running, and the line between those points was not constructed for a speed much over 40mph. 'This accident and the evidence given at the inquiry point as to the desirability of providing a different class of engine for express trains running at high speed.'

14 APRIL, 1864

Ellen Reynolds died at the Truro infirmary. Before her death she made a statement to the surgeon and a police constable about the circumstances in which her companion, Elizabeth Grose, had already been killed. They had been working at a gunpowder factory in the city and were ordered to leave the premises at dusk. Disobeying orders, they worked several additional hours without permission, then entered the granulating house, locked themselves in and lay down on the floor to sleep. There was some powder in the house undergoing preparatory drying, and it was the duty of the watchman to turn it at intervals during the night. He asked the girls if they would turn it for him, as they were partly undressed and he did not like to enter. At 5.30 a.m. he told them it was time to get up, and shortly afterwards a boy who was also on the watch told them to hurry as the kettle was boiling in the boiler house. When the explosion occurred a little later, Miss Grose was killed immediately, while Miss Reynolds was standing in the doorway, where she was enveloped in flames and blown forwards.

15 APRIL, 1936

Martin Luther Grose, Stanley Phillips, Clifford Edward Trethewey, Albert James John Clarke, and Arthur Gerald Neal, all of Nanpean, were brought before the magistrates at Tregony. They had been charged with stealing about 800 Lent lilies between them, the property of Robert Alexander Harvey, of Grampound Road, Nanpean, and all pleaded guilty. Con Kersey said that Grose had 11½ dozen lilies, valued at 3s 10d, Philips 9 dozen, worth 3s, Neal 15½ dozen, worth 5s 2d, Trethewey 13 dozen, worth 4s 4d, and Clarke 17 dozen, worth 5s 8d. The defendants expressed regret for what they had done, explaining that they were from the clay area, and thought they were entitled to pick the flowers. Fining them *2s 6d* each, the Chairman of the Magistrates told them, 'You ought to respect the beauties of nature, and leave them where they are, instead of entering private ground and preying upon them in this way.'

16 APRIL, 1904

Dr Vinter of Torpoint (*see* 25 March) was driving home in his trap after visiting patients in Antony and St John's, accompanied by a boy, Crossley. Near the end of Borough Farm Lane, a motorcyclist came along behind and, before the doctor could pull over, he dashed up and suddenly passed in front of them. The frightened horse kicked away the front of the trap and one of the shafts. Dr Vinter shouted at the cyclist to stop, but the latter took no notice. The horse got its legs clear, and bolted just after passing Antony Lodge gates, and the doctor was pitched out, striking his head. Crossley stayed in the trap until the horse neared Coomber Park, then jumped out, unharmed. Mr Bardford, who was passing at the time, drew his wagon in close to the hedge in order to stop the runaway horse, and Mr Granger drove Vinter and Crossley home. The former was slightly injured but recovered after a couple of days, while the latter was merely suffering from shock, but the badly injured horse had to be destroyed.

17 APRIL, 1928

Charles Mutton (27) of St Blazey, employed by Messrs Anderson and Rowlands, amusement caterers, was killed near Ivybridge. He tried to jump onto the bar connecting the engine of one of the lorries as they were proceeding along the main road, and fell off. One of the wheels of the lorry passed over his head, and death was instantaneous.

18 APRIL, 1892

Two Irishmen were sentenced for a brutal and unprovoked assault on another man at Camborne; one was given a two-month sentence and the other six weeks. After the case the prisoners, still accompanied by the police, were followed through the streets by an excited crowd who struck and threw stones at them. An Irishman who had given evidence for the prisoners was attacked and flung into a sawpit. He was taken out covered in blood, and a large newly-sharpened knife was also recovered from the pit. The Irishmen's quarters were also attacked and wrecked. The mob subsequently went to Cook's Kitchen Mine, about a mile from the town, where they savagely ill-treated an Irishman at work. When they returned to the town they attacked the Roman Catholic church, smashed in the windows, broke open the doors, and did much damage inside. The image of the Virgin Mary was torn down, flung into the road and trampled underfoot, while the altar, gas fittings, seats and organ were completely destroyed. The house of Father McKey, the Catholic priest, was next singled out for attack, and he only saved himself by scaling a wall in order to evade his pursuers. Next to suffer was the house of Major Pike, a prominent member of the local Roman Catholic community, whose conservatory was destroyed. By 10 p.m. the town was reported to be completely in the hands of the mob, the police apparently powerless to quell the disturbance.

Next day the magistrates issued an order requiring all public houses in the town to close at 4 p.m., and advised all residents to remain within their houses during the evening as far as possible. By midnight the excitement was subsiding, and the mob was almost under control, but a small crowd assembled and pelted the police, who were ordered to clear the streets. In the rush that ensued, several persons were trampled on and injured. A few roughs went 'on an expedition' to Brea, but returned to Camborne without having done any harm.

19 APRIL 1940

Mrs Sarah Jane Blatchford, of Hendra Bridge, Liskeard, was walking towards town when, near the farm entrance to Luxstowe, a gust of wind caught a box she was carrying under her right arm and she lost her balance. She fell into the path of an agricultural tractor driven by Mr Ernest Ough, who was going in the same direction. She fell between the front and rear nearside wheels, and one wheel passed over her. The driver was astonished when she rose to her feet unaided afterwards. First aid was given by a Girl Guide from the Liskeard Guide Hut. She was taken to the town's cottage hospital, where an X-ray failed to reveal any serious injury, but she was detained for a while as she was suffering from shock and external scratching and bruising. The main weight of the wheel was thought to have been absorbed by her handbag.

20 APRIL 1918

An inquest was held on the bodies of two children, aged 4½ and 5½, who died in a fire the previous day at Tresco. They had been sleeping in the upper room of a cottage, which was found to be engulfed in flames soon after midnight. The stairs were inaccessible, and attempts were made to reach the youngsters through the window. Eventually a neighbour managed to get in, extricated them and passed them to a doctor, but by then both were dead. The house was entirely burnt out. At the inquest a verdict of death by suffocation was returned.

21 APRIL, 1923

The bodies of Annie Trenberth Osborne (48), a widow, and her daughter Ann Trenberth (15), were found on a blood-soaked bed in their house at Union Row, St Teath. A few weeks earlier it had been evident to the villagers that young Ann was expecting a baby. Her condition was not discussed openly, least of all by her mother, a proud and private person, who must have been shocked beyond measure by her child's lapse from virtue.

On Easter Sunday the girl was taken ill at church and escorted home by the vicar's wife. She refused all offers of help, and insisted that no doctor should be called. When she was next seen a few days later she was clearly no longer pregnant, but looked terribly ill. Two doctors, sent to the house by worried villagers, examined her and confirmed she had recently given birth – but there was no clue as to what might have happened to the baby. The doctors' visit seemed to throw Annie into a panic, and once they had left, she was seen running round the house, bolting the doors and boarding up the windows.

A day or so later worried neighbours knocked on Annie's door, but could get no answer. Annie's brother, Aaron Ede, and the anxious party finally gained access to the house and made the gruesome discovery. The conclusion drawn at the inquest was that Annie was so ashamed of her daughter that she had cut the girl's throat and then taken her own life. The house and gardens were searched, but no trace of a baby's body was ever found.

The grave of Annie Trenberth Osborne and her daughter Ann at the Church of St Tetha and St Teath. (© Nicola Sly)

22 APRIL, 1820

A boy named Hosking was working in Dolcoath Mine, while a man alongside him was preparing to blast a hole in a damp part of the rock. He took up part of a tin tube to use as a fuse, but did not know that it contained powder at the time. He tried to look at the candle through it, came too close, and the powder exploded. The tube was driven through his eye into his head, and he was killed instantly.

23 APRIL, 1850

At West Caradon Mine, James Clemo (15) was rolling some materials underground. As he arrived at the plot to deposit it, he was about to take the candle from the fore part of the barrow which he had emptied, and put one foot in it to do so, when it overturned, throwing him down the shaft, a depth of 104 fathoms. The remains of his mutilated body were collected and taken to his home. At the inquest a verdict of accidental death was returned.

24 APRIL, 1961

The body of Eric Pengelly (59) of Fore Street, Calstock, sexton and bell ringer of St Andrew's Church, was examined by Dr Denis Hocking. He had collapsed and died while ringing the church bells for evensong on the previous day, and evensong was cancelled as a result. As it was proved he had died of heart failure, it was decided there would be no need for an inquest.

25 APRIL, 1862

Nathaniel Cole was placed in the stocks for six hours at Camelford for not paying a fine of 5s and 5s costs, recently imposed for being drunk and riotous. On the same day James Bawden was placed in the stocks at Foundry Square, Hayle, for similar offences. The last recorded use of stocks in the county was at Camborne in 1866.

26 APRIL: Jamaica Inn Ghost Stories

On this day in 1989 the funeral of Daphne du Maurier, one of Cornwall's best-loved novelists of the twentieth century, was held close to the family home at Menabilly. Jamaica Inn on Bodmin Moor, immortalised in her novel of the same name and published in 1936, is associated with many tales of murder, treachery and scandal.

Hayle.

*Jamaica Inn,
Bodmin Moor.*

One tells of a strange man who stood at the bar drinking from a tankard, when he was called outside by others to attend to business – and never returned. He was savagely murdered and his battered body was later found a few miles away on the moor, but the case was never solved. Ever since then, people have reported hearing his footsteps as he returned to the bar to finish his ale.

Other ghost tales of the inn tell of a figure of a highwayman in a tricorn hat, of a young mother and her baby, and of the spirit of a young smuggler who was killed and is said to sit motionless, dressed in old-fashioned seaman's clothes, on a wall in the courtyard.

Quay Street, Penzance. (© Christine Matthews, www.geograph.org.uk)

27 APRIL, 1942

Alfred Nicholas Harvey of Quay Street, Penzance, was charged at Penzance Borough Justices with assault and inflicting grievous bodily harm on his wife Gertrude. Evidence showed that the defendant tried to strangle his wife after alleging that she was associating with soldiers. He had been invalided out of the army. Several previous convictions were reported against the defendant, but none since 1929. The magistrates ordered him to be bound over in the sum of £5 for twelve months.

28 APRIL: St Winwaloe and the Penfolds

The Church of St Winwaloe in the rural parish of Poundstock, near Widemouth Bay, has had an unfortunate history. During the fourteenth century there was bitter rivalry between a gang of robbers and pirates, who regularly attacked ships sailing off Widemouth Bay. The Revd William Penfound, who was believed to be a member or at least a close associate of the pirates, fell foul of the robbers. In 1357 several of them burst in on him while he was officiating at a service in the church and hacked him to death at the altar. Ever since then, it is said, his ghost has haunted St Winwaloe's.

Not long afterwards another vicar was sentenced to life imprisonment for his part in a murder, and in the sixteenth century another was hanged for leading a rebellion against the changes being made in the Book of Common Prayer.

Two more members of the Penfound family, who lived at Penfound Manor, also came to a tragic end during the Civil War. They were staunch Royalists and Kate, one of the daughters, fell in love with John Trebarfoot of Trebarfoot Manor. As the Trebarfoots were Parliamentarians, she knew her father, Arthur, would never agree to their marriage, and so she decided to elope. One evening she climbed down a ladder from her bedroom window to the courtyard, where John was waiting for her. However, Arthur Penfound had discovered their plan and was lying in wait for them, and tried to prevent them from leaving. Swords were drawn and in the ensuing

St Winwaloe Church, Poundstock, said to be haunted by the ghost of Revd William Poundstock. (© Alan G. Simkins)

struggle John Trebarfoot was killed instantly, while father and daughter both later died from their wounds.

29 APRIL, 1936

At East Kerrier Sessions, Penryn, Albert James Tozer, a farmer, pleaded guilty of failing to record the movement of five pigs from Helston Market to his premises. Superintendent Norish said that the pigs came from premises which were later certified as being infected by the outbreak of swine fever in West Cornwall at the time and the authorities were concerned. The Bench fined the defendant £2 10s.

At the same proceedings, Thomas Laity Stephens, of Constantine, pleaded guilty of failing to boil bones and other parts of carcasses before feeding them to his pigs. He was fined 10s.

30 APRIL, 1882

After an outbreak of smallpox among the Devon & Cornwall Light Infantry at Bodmin Barracks, the War Office gave orders that the 3rd Battalion, which was to have assembled there the following day for its annual twenty-seven days' training, would proceed to Devonport and be accommodated at Crownhill Fort, Plymouth. The officer commanding the 32nd Regimental District was instructed to take measures to prevent men from going to Bodmin, and to see that all men arriving at the station would not be allowed to leave until they were on the train to Devonport.

MAY

The funeral procession at St Mary's for victims of the liner Schiller, wrecked off the Isles of Scilly on 7 May 1875 with the loss of 335 lives.

1 MAY 1906

Two sisters, the Misses Gribble, of Trago Mills, Liskeard, were returning home after having been out stalking rabbits. After crossing the River Fowey by Bodithiel Bridge, they were within 70yds of home when one of them, who was a few yards in front, was attacked by an abnormally large badger. She ran away, dodging behind trees as she took aim with her gun. Not until she had fired a third bullet 'was her furious antagonist placed *hors de combat*'.

2 MAY 1872

John Kitto was killed at Drakewalls Mine. While he was walking across the tramway, a large stone fell from the open shaft above him, hit him on the head, and he died at once. He left a widow and eight children.

At the inquest at Callington, Captain Gregory, on behalf of the mine management, said that he had been unwell for some time and therefore unable to inspect the shafts to ensure they were properly boarded. He had given orders for it to be done, but in the place where the accident occurred, it had been neglected, and there was an open space of ten fathoms left untimbered. During the last two or three years there had been several accidents in the mine, some fatal. A newspaper correspondent noted that, in this case, a little timber properly placed would have prevented the accident. It was surely time for a miners' inspection bill, though he feared it would 'not be until working men, in counties where mines usually are, are privileged with the franchise.'

3 MAY 1928

Alfred John Martin and Alfred Salt both pleaded guilty at Liskeard Magistrates' Court to breaking and entering a house at Hannafore, Looe, where they stole clothing, two watches and a chain valued together at £13 1s 6d, the property of Mr T. Septimus Putland, a hotel proprietor.

Hannafore, Looe.

Superintendent Drew said that Putland went away for the weekend, and when he returned on the evening of Monday 30 April, he found his premises had been entered by means of a ladder at the upstairs window, and the articles were missing. He reported the theft to Constable Cortis, who, along with Sergeant Prust of Pelynt, traced the goods to the defendants. Their task was made easier after Salt had offered one of the watches to a local jeweller. They confessed to the theft, and indicated where they had concealed the articles. The charge was reduced to one of larceny. Salt was sentenced to fourteen days' imprisonment and Martin, who had previous convictions, to one month.

4 MAY 1897

Richard Hawke and Henry Northcott, wagoners, of Northill, appeared at Launceston County Petty Sessions, charged with leaving large stones on the highway at Lewannick. Both men pleaded guilty. The Bench asked them to pay 1s 2d, the total court costs, cautioned them that it was a dangerous practice, and asked the press to make full notice of it in their reports in order to try and deter others from doing the same. At the same court, Richard Prout was fined 2s for allowing his cattle to stray.

5 MAY 1841

During the evening, after work, Mr Withell, a Padstow shipbuilder, and seven of his workforce, took their gig and rowed to Newland Island, off Pentire Head, Padstow Bay, in search of gulls' eggs. On getting into the boat, the lift of the sea raised the gig onto a projecting rock, the tide then fell about 10ft immediately afterwards, causing the vessel to capsize. Five of the men saved themselves with some difficulty by getting onto the island. However, James Docton, son of Mr Docton, a local printer, and John Brenton, were both drowned. The former left a wife and one child, the latter a wife and four

Newland Island, off Pentire Head, Padstow. (© Barry Hodges)

children. The boat was dashed to pieces, and the others were stranded on the island for several hours, calling for help until a passing vessel spotted them and took them back to the mainland.

6 MAY 1915

An inquest was held at St Blazey Gate on the death of Francis John Rowse (35), a greengrocer. His mother, Eliza, said that on the morning of 5 May she called to him while he was upstairs, but there was no answer. She went to his bedroom and found him lying dead on the floor with a severe wound to his throat, and a razor by his side. He had had a serious illness thirteen years previously, and had been subject to depression ever since. Dr Goldie had been to visit him and left the house only about ten minutes earlier. A verdict of 'suicide while temporarily insane' was returned.

7 MAY 1875

The German transatlantic liner *Schiller*, built on the Clyde two years earlier, was wrecked off the Isles of Scilly. She had left New York for Hamburg via Plymouth on 27 April carrying a general cargo, 250 bags of mail and a large quantity of gold pieces, with an estimated value of £100,000.

During the evening of 7 May they encountered thick fog, and the ship reduced her speed to four knots. Without warning she struck Retallier Ledges at about 10 p.m. The engines reversed, and the ship was pulled clear, but heavy sea caught her broadside and sent her grinding onto the rocks. Signal guns were fired to call for assistance, but the sound was misunderstood, and thought to be the normal arrival signal for a ship approaching the islands. There was a birthday party on board in one of the officers' cabins at the time, and passengers were panicking so much that the captain fired two revolver shots over their heads to try and keep order, but it had little effect. Only two lifeboats were launched successfully, with twenty-six women and one man reaching Tresco safely. Of the other six lifeboats, two were crushed when the funnel fell on top of them, two were jammed in launching gear owing to the list of the ship, one was marked against the ship's side as it was being lowered, and one capsized into the sea.

Of the 372 people on board, only thirty-seven survived, and 335 drowned. Many of the bodies were never found. Over a hundred were buried in the churchyard at Old Town, in plain deal coffins painted black and laid in mass graves. Many of the women who had been washed ashore were still dressed in all their finery. Newly-wed Louise Holzmaister (23) was sailing to be reunited with her millionaire husband, and her body was never recovered. Her grieving husband erected a monument to her in Old Town churchyard.

8 MAY 1872

The sufferings of Ann Kitto (25), of Breage, came to an end. On the evening of Sunday 25 April, she had complained of pain in her side. Her mother applied turpentine cloths to the affected part. When this produced no relief, Mrs Kitto attempted using a mustard potion. There was a lighted candle by the side of the bed, near which turpentine cloths were left. While Mrs Kitto was downstairs she heard a scream, and ran upstairs to find Ann on the floor, on her knees, with her clothes in flames. Mrs Kitto tried to put them out, but Ann was severely burned around the chest and throat. A neighbour, Johanna Andrew, called round, and said that Ann had knocked the candlestick over while turning round the bed. Her condition gradually worsened over the next fortnight until she finally succumbed. Mrs Kitto was too ill to give evidence at the inquest, which returned a verdict of accidental death.

9 MAY 1941

Mrs Muriel Lean, of Tregonissey Road, St Austell, was charged with theft at St Austell Magistrates' Court. For the prosecution, Inspector Cobbledick said two sailors met two women at the Sun Inn, and they later went to a dance at the town hall. At 10.45 p.m. Mrs Lean asked one of the sailors for a cigarette. He said he had none, so she offered to get some. He gave her a 10s note to pay for the cigarettes, and she promptly ran out of the dance hall with it. Mrs Lean was found guilty, fined £5, with 15s 6d costs, and ordered to hand the money back.

10 MAY 1892

Mary Elizabeth Heard (6), daughter of labourer Samuel Heard, was a pupil at Poughill National School, Stratton. Whilst playing outside between lessons Mary began quarrelling with Ellen Mitchell, described as 'a deserted child', who was about the same age. Ellen hit Mary once or twice on the head with a slate, and when Mary later complained of feeling sick, she was sent home. She returned to school in the afternoon, but by the evening she was suffering from violent diarrhoea, and had severe convulsions. A neighbour called in to help and Mary's father went to Stratton to fetch Dr Braund. The doctor came to examine Mary at home, but she was sickening and died at around midnight.

11 MAY 1937

Grace Howe (77) and her son John (49) were found dead in their cottage at The Square, Gunnislake. Grace's granddaughter, Myrtle Gibson (18), had gone to have dinner with her grandmother, but when she knocked she received no answer. She went and told her father, Ernest Gibson, who came out to have a look. He noticed blood on the upstairs window and called Constable Deacon, who forced an entrance through the window. He found Grace in bed, her throat cut, the bedclothes saturated with blood, and John lying face down at the foot of the bed, also in a pool of blood; both were quite obviously dead. The door was locked from inside, so nobody else could have entered the house.

An inquest was held on 13 May at the town hall where, it was said, 'the coronation decorations [for King George VI and Queen Elizabeth, crowned on 12 May] looked out of place.' It was established that John had killed his mother and then taken his own life. A bachelor, John had served in the First World War with the Royal Artillery in India, Mesopotamia and France, and was wounded in action. He had then found employment as a quarry labourer, but had to leave his work as he needed to care full-time for his mother, who was by then virtually bedridden. Neighbours described him as 'a hard-working, clean-living fellow' who had nursed his mother devotedly and waited on her hand and foot for some years, and done all the housework on his own. Only a few hours before the discovery of the bodies, he had been seen in the street, and appeared to be his usual cheery, uncomplaining self.

12 MAY 1938

An inquest was held into the death of Joseph Floyd (34), of Church Street, Crowan. He had been killed on 10 May when his friend's gun accidentally went off as he was climbing over a hedge. Reginald Sparks, of Praze, said that Floyd had invited him for an hour's shooting, and he put two cartridges in his gun before leaving the house. He had only started shooting only a fortnight earlier and had never handled a gun before that. He was certain the weapon was not cocked when he left home. They crossed over two fields, and when reaching the hedge Floyd went over first. Sparks followed him closely behind, and had his left knee and left hand on the hedge. He was holding the gun in his right hand, his knee struck the butt and the weapon went off. Floyd was only 3ft from the barrel of the gun at the time. He fell and was bleeding badly. Sparks ran through the fields to fetch the police and a doctor, and then returned to Floyd, pulled off his shirt and then his vest to try and plug the wound, but to no avail.

Floyd was taken to Redruth Hospital. The main part of the charge had lodged in the right lobe of the liver, which was lacerated beyond repair. The wound was, at point of entry, only a little larger than the barrel of the shotgun, thus all the shot had entered the wound. Death was due to shock and haemorrhage from liver injuries.

13 MAY 1946

Edith Lovell, a domestic servant, of The Terrace, Penzance, was charged with having obtained £3 by a forged Post Office Savings Bank withdrawal on demand receipt on 18 August 1942, and a similar sum on 11 December 1942. She was sentenced to four months' imprisonment.

14 MAY 1913

There was a heavy thunderstorm at Polperro at about 5 p.m. Mr Geach, a postman, was riding his bicycle at the bottom of Langreek Hill, and was struck by lightning. He lost control of the bicycle, was thrown heavily, and remained in a dazed condition for several minutes. After recovering he walked to the post office as his cycle had been badly damaged, finished his work for the day, and then went to Dr Hutchinson's surgery, where stitches were inserted in a cut over his right eye. At nearby Crumplehorn, an outhouse was badly damaged, and several panes of glass in the school windows were broken. Nobody was injured, as the children were on their Whitsun holiday. A dog in a slaughterhouse died after being struck by lightning, while several fishing and pleasure boats at sea were at risk of being swamped by large waves.

Langreek Hill, Polperro.

15 MAY 1868

An inquest was held on the death of Maria Stickland, a little girl who had lived near Hayle, and who was found drenched with blood on the bed where she had been sleeping with her father. She had been dead for some time. Near her was the body of her father John, who was close to death himself. Blood was flowing from a large wound in his throat, which was promptly sewn up and bandaged by a surgeon. A bloodstained razor was found under a pillow. Only two days earlier Mrs Stickland had died of consumption. The family of three had always lived happily together, and Mr Stickland was devoted to his wife and child. Apart from having once asked those around him if his little girl was dead, he had made no reference to the crime which he had obviously committed. Because he was undergoing such mental suffering, the police did not allow him to attend the inquest. The only witness called, Benjamin Harris, Mr Stickland's hairdresser, confirmed that the razor found in the bedroom was the same which he had sharpened for the prisoner on the Friday prior to the murder. The jury returned a verdict of wilful murder against Mr Stickland, and a warrant was made out for his committal to the next assizes.

16 MAY 1643

A battle was fought in the morning about half a mile north of Stratton. Reaching the town first on 15 May, the Parliamentary commander, the Earl of Stamford, had deployed his troops on the summit of a substantial hill which still bears his name. Although his men were outnumbered almost two to one Sir Ralph Hopton, the Royalist commander, chose to attack this formidable position, taking advantage of the absence of the Parliamentarian horse. In a hard-fought clash of arms, the tactical superiority of the Royalist force carried the day against what appeared to be overwhelming odds. Three hundred soldiers in the Parliamentarians' force were killed, and as they fled the field an estimated 1,500 or more prisoners were captured, as was a substantial amount of artillery.

Sir Ralph Hopton, who commanded the Royalist forces at the Battle of Stratton in 1643.

Looe harbour, where a fisherman was lost after a crabbing expedition on 17 May 1906.

17 MAY 1906

Two fishermen, Mr Sanders and Mr Medland (72), were working off the coast at Looe. They were returning from crabbing in their sailing boat, and bearing down for their store pots between Looe Island and the harbour entrance. At the same time a steam tug from Fowey, *Countess of Jersey*, was leaving the harbour, having in tow two light schooners, *Mary Sinclair* and *Emily Millington*, proceeding to Fowey to load china clay. The fishermen did not see that one of the schooners had a boat in tow, and though they cleared the vessels, they came into collision with the boat, which cut right into them, and sank their boat at once. Sanders was rescued, but Medland had become entangled with the sails and sank with the boat.

18 MAY 1954

William Terry (20), of Antony, was charged at Torpoint Magistrates' Court with causing bodily harm to two boys, both aged 13. When he pleaded guilty Mr D.B. Peacock, Chairman of the Bench, advised him to find some companions of his own age.

Superintendent B. Johns said that Terry was in the habit of throwing stones at a camp which some of the boys had built near a garage yard. On the evening of 7 April he entered the yard with a girl and began throwing stones without any provocation. One boy, William Tucker, was struck on the head and received a wound 1½in across. The other, William Lobb, was struck on the head as he tried to run for cover. When questioned about the incident, Terry admitted throwing stones, but said he was 'just skylarking about.' An agricultural engineer by profession, he had formerly served with the Devonshire Regiment in the Middle East. He apologised for his dangerous behaviour but the Chairman told him that such actions could not be excused, and fined him £1.

19 MAY 1862

An inquest was held at Bodmin Land, in the parish of St Ive, on the death of Angelina Honeychurch (3), daughter of William Honeychurch, a miner. She had been slightly unwell for several weeks, but her parents did not think her ill enough to merit medical attention. Early on the morning of 18 May, as her mother was getting her dressed, the little girl suddenly felt faint and was dead within a few minutes.

20 MAY 1975

Dame Barbara Hepworth (72), one of the most renowned sculptors of the age, died in a fire at Trewyn Studio, St Ives, which she had purchased in 1949 and made her home ever since. She had been suffering from throat cancer and the effects of a thigh injury for some years. Her night nurse, Mrs Rosetta Macmin, arrived to find her very tired and left her to go to bed by herself. Later she thought she smelt burning plastic and went into Dame Barbara's first-floor bedroom to find her, the bed, and even the telephone on fire. She ran for help, and several neighbours came in, climbed the stairs but were unable to enter the room as they were beaten back by flames and dense fumes. Peter Lethbridge, a local teacher, made three attempts to enter the room, and on the last occasion he was carried out in a state of virtual collapse. The house lights had failed and it was impossible to reach Dame Barbara until the flames had been subdued.

She had been in the habit of smoking in bed, although her staff had warned her of the risk, and at the inquest at Penzance on 30 July, it was suggested that she had fallen asleep and accidentally set light to her bedclothes with a cigarette in her hand.

21 MAY 1948

Two fires were reported in different parts of the county. The Penzance Fire Brigade was called out to extinguish a fire at Morvah, where peat underneath the gorse had been set alight and was threatening a cottage, and spent seven hours fighting it. The flames were not under control until about 4 p.m. In Penzance itself, a county council storage depot was the scene of a fire which broke out in the timber store, and Helston Fire Brigade was called.

22 MAY 1884

An inquest was held at Liskeard into the sudden death of William England, who had been the ostler, or stableman, at the Sportsman's Arms, Menheniot. At about 7 a.m. he had been going out of the back door when he had a violent fit of coughing, burst a blood vessel, and fell dead almost at once. A verdict of death from natural causes was returned.

23 MAY 1902

Mabel Morrison (18), of Falmouth, was charged on 28 May with stealing a skirt worth 3s 6d from Annie Roberts, a second-hand clothes dealer at King Street, Plymouth. Morrison had entered the shop on the afternoon of 23 May, and asked to be allowed to go and do her hair up in a bedroom, behind the door of which the skirt was hanging. She returned on 24 May, and slept for a while in a chair in the kitchen. While Annie Roberts was attending to a customer, Mabel took the skirt, went out and sold it to Mrs Sarah Luke of King Street, saying it was her property. She was arrested at the Salvation Army Hostel, King Street, by Constable Edwards, and told him that she had sold it to get money for food, as she had not eaten for three or four days. She pleaded guilty and apologised. In court Constable Sowerby said she should be remanded pending enquiries.

Morrison's parents lived in Falmouth, and her father was a coal porter. She had been in Plymouth for five months, three of which had been spent at the Salvation Army Hostel, where she was known as very troublesome. A situation had been obtained for her as a domestic servant, but she left voluntarily after a disagreement with the mistress's daughter. When she committed the theft she was destitute. She had previously served two months' imprisonment at Bodmin for a similar offence. The chairman said she would be remanded in custody while they contacted her parents.

24 MAY 1922

George Ellis (64) of Hayle had been taken ill while taking a walk along Penzance seafront during the evening of 23 May. He was rushed to the West Cornwall Infirmary, but next morning he died of heart failure.

25 MAY 1896

Three young men hired a sailing boat at Penzance. About 100yds from the mouth at Newlyn harbour, they tried to turn the boat around, when it capsized. Fishermen nearby tried to put out rescue boats for them and one of the youths, John Stevens, was rescued, but both his companions were drowned.

The Fish Quay, Newlyn.

26 MAY: Fighting Cocks, Saltash

The Fighting Cocks at Saltash was an inn in the late eighteenth century which had a notorious reputation as the place where ne'er-do-wells plotted their misdeeds under the approving eye of an evil landlord. A servant girl set off from Plymouth with a bundle of clothes and her savings to visit friends in Callington. She was seen in Saltash, and would have gone past the inn – but was never seen again. People at the inn were suspected of being involved in, if not responsible for, her disappearance, but nothing was proved.

A few years later, as the landlord lay dying, he shouted, 'Take her away! Take her away! I meant her no harm!' Those around him assumed that the girl's death must have been very much on his conscience. Some years later when the inn was demolished in order to widen the road, a skeleton thought to be that of the missing girl was found buried on the site.

27 MAY 1887

The steamer *Castleford*, a 3,044-ton vessel laden with 450 cattle, was bound for London from Montreal when it ran aground in thick fog on Great Crebawethan, Western Rocks. The eighteen cattlemen on board offered the Scillonians £2 for every animal they could help to rescue alive and put safely onto the island of Annet. Some were successfully landed, but then the vessel broke in two, and disappeared before the operation could be completed. Many of the cattle were drowned, and their carcasses drifted ashore for months afterwards.

28 MAY 1850

Over 3,000 spectators came to watch the annual wrestling at St Austell on 28 and 29 May. An accident occurred when the booth belonging to Mr Ball of the Golden Lion Inn, and Mr Jones who lived in the town suffered a broken leg. A contemporary press report assured its readers, 'we are glad to say it can be easily replaced as it was only a wooden one'.

29 MAY 1899

At Truro Police Court James Harvey and Travers Lonsdale, two mining students, were charged with animal cruelty. On 26 May they had been seen in Harrison Terrace, Truro, with three dogs. When a cat ran across the road Harvey set the dogs on it, and it was so badly mutilated that Sergeant Scantlebury had to put it out of its misery. The defendants saw the dogs savaging the cat, but were seen to go away instead of calling them off. Lonsdale said that neither of the dogs belonged to him, and as he had not set them on the cat he did not consider it his duty to try and stop them. When Mr Trevail, the magistrate, asked him if he would not have 'regarded it as an act of humanity to try and get the dogs off,' Lonsdale shrugged. 'I don't know,' he said, 'they are not my dogs.' Trevail asked if he did not consider it his duty to stop cruelty of that sort, but Lonsdale replied he 'did not think about it.' The mayor said that both defendants were by birth, education and culture no doubt gentlemen, but their conduct in this case was neither gentle nor manly. The magistrates considered Harvey and Lonsdale equally responsible, but as no technical responsibility could be proved, Lonsdale would be discharged. Harvey was fined the maximum sum of £5 and costs, or three months' hard labour. They were warned that if they were brought before the court on a similar matter again, they would be sentenced to imprisonment without the option of a fine.

30 MAY 1939

The Revd Walter Edward Guest, a former vicar of St Austell, was sentenced to seventeen months' imprisonment at Dorset Assizes, Dorchester, for an offence involving 'lewd conduct' committed with William Chester Trelease (21), a painter, who was bound over. Guest was vicar of St John's Church, Portland, at the time, and was married with one child and a stepson of 20. His counsel said he was now completely ruined and pleaded for him to be allowed to go to a home for treatment.

31 MAY 1833

Mr Butters was floating on a balk of timber on the Liskeard canal while he was drunk. He lost his footing, fell in and was drowned.

JUNE

A mid-nineteenth-century view of Helston, where William Pascoe threatened to burn his house down on 30 June 1872.

1 JUNE 1929

At Falmouth Police Court, sailors William Hobbs and Harold Elvy pleaded not guilty to wilfully neglecting to join the steamer *Valega* after each received advance notes of £4 each. Mr Jocelyn Ratcliffe, representing the Shipping Federation, said that the men were due to join the ship at midnight on Wednesday 29 May, but failed to do so. Elvy informed the Bench that after he had received advance warning, he went to his home at Penzance to get some of his kit. He missed his last train to Falmouth, as the bus went no further than Helston. Hobbs said he went to the docks thinking that the boat conveying the crew left there instead of the town quay. He asked that the docks police should be communicated with to prove the truth of his story. The Bench sent for Sergeant Collins of the docks police, who confirmed Hobbs' statement. The court gave them both the benefit of the doubt, and discharged them after they promised to repay the money advanced to them.

2 JUNE 1898

Albert Jenner (22) was charged at Penzance Police Court with wounding John Nieve, skipper of the Lowestoft fishing boat *Constance*. Jenner, of another Lowestoft boat, *Marguerite*, had an argument with Nieve while they were at Newlyn, and struck him several times with a pocket knife, wounding him on the face, arms and back. Inspector Cull said that Nieve

Fishermen's cottages at Newlyn, c. 1890.

was not yet well enough to come and give evidence in court. The prisoner was remanded for a further hearing on Monday 6 June.

3 JUNE 1857

On this date Samuel Woolcock of Kenwyn, Isaac Bennett, and Thomas Goog, all of Kea, assaulted Walter Tippet, toll collector at Redruth Gate. The prisoners were horse jockeys, returning from Camborne Fair, held the previous day. As they came back shortly after midnight, at first they refused to pay the toll. At length Bennett and Goog agreed to do so, but Woolcock refused, and struck Tippet with his stick, then threw him to the ground. The collector was a much stronger man, and was about to get up off the ground, when Bennett and Goog both kicked him and held him down while Woolcock ran away. They were soon apprehended, and later appeared before the magistrates. Bennett and Goog were fined £3 each and costs, Woolcock £1 and costs.

4 JUNE 1928

James Thomas, a taxi driver of Grove Cottage, Falmouth, was charged with dangerous driving in the town. He had been driving from Greenbank to Prince Street at a considerable pace, when he took his hands off the wheel and held them up in the air. The vehicle veered onto the wrong side of the road, and had there been any other vehicles around there would almost certainly have been an accident. Dr Banks and another witness gave evidence, but the defendant denied the offence and said he had gone onto the wrong side of the road so he could see around the corner. He admitted having been cautioned later in the day for driving without his hands on the wheel, and was fined £3.

5 JUNE 1870

A fire broke out at Falmouth at about 3 a.m. and resulted in the total destruction of eight or nine waterside houses before it was brought under control. It started in the back premises belonging to Mr Webber, a baker and confectioner, in Market Street. Spreading quickly north and south, it took only four hours to destroy property estimated at a value of between £20,000 and £30,000, including the stock-in-trade and furniture of Mr Fox, ironmonger; Mr Goach, draper; Mr Richards, bookseller; Mr Kelway, grocer; Mr Turner, tailor; Mr Harvey, grocer; and others. The fire brigades of Falmouth, Penryn, and Truro, the latter summoned by telegraph, as well as those of the *Ganges* training ship and Pendennis, with a detachment of artillery, were soon on the spot, and rendered most effective service, keeping perfect order all the time. One or two houses had to be pulled down to prevent the fire from spreading any further.

6 JUNE 1378

Robert Tresilian was knighted and at around the same time appointed Justice of the King's Bench. Sometimes called 'Cornwall's worst contribution to justice', he was born in 1340 at Tresilian House, near Newquay and as a young man he went to London, studied law and was appointed a judge. In 1380, shortly after the first poll tax was levied, he was appointed Lord Chief Justice of England. Within six months of the Peasants' Revolt he had condemned 1,500 peasants to hang for non-payment. Although he remained a favourite of King Richard II for a while, he fell from favour when he took part in a parliamentary commission to review and control the royal finances, something which the king regarded as an infringement on his prerogative. He was later involved in a case of espionage against the Duke of Gloucester, a dissident nobleman. For several days he recorded the comings and goings of the duke's visitors, but was then recognised, arrested and summoned to appear at court at Westminster. In February 1388, when his case came up for trial, he was found heavily disguised in hiding at Westminster Abbey, where he tried to claim sanctuary. A mob dragged him into court, and as he had already been convicted of treason, he was taken to Tyburn where he was hanged upside down in chains.

7 JUNE 1948

Mr and Mrs C.H. Turner, aged about 55 and 45 respectively, lived at Tonbridge and arrived at Porthleven on their honeymoon on 5 June. On this day they went for a swim at the notorious danger spot Tye Rocks near Falmouth. Although they were warned that the sea was particularly rough, they

Tresilian House, near Newquay, birthplace of Sir Robert Tresilian in 1378.

insisted that they were strong swimmers, and would come to no harm. They would have done well to listen, for both were drowned.

8 JUNE 1846

Hylton's travelling menagerie arrived at Redruth, and the evening's performance drew a crowd of several thousand of all ages. At about 10 p.m. some lads began teasing a blind hyena, which in its irritation went and picked a fight with another hyena in the same cage. This aroused a lion, who was in an equally bad mood and roared loudly. The spectators were terrified when the lion broke loose. Panic set in and everyone rushed for the entrance, with the elderly and the very young, those least able to fend for themselves, thrown down and trampled on. People ran along the nearby streets, into private houses, fearful that the animals would catch and attack them. The surgeons were summoned to help those suffering from severe bruising and shock. Nobody was killed although, according to the first reports about twenty-four hours later, 'it can scarcely be said that all the sufferers are out of danger.'

9 JUNE 1878

Edward Spender (47), editor of the *Western Morning News*, and his two eldest sons, Reginald (13) and Sydney (11), went for a walk to Tregonhawke Cove, Whitsands, and then a bathe. Within five minutes of entering the water, all three had disappeared beneath the waves. Russell Rendle, Spender's brother-in-law, had been walking with them but preferred to watch from the rocks rather than go swimming. He ran the two miles to the coastguard station to raise the alarm. The boys' bodies were washed up on the shore on the evening of 22 June, a mile eastwards of the point at which they were last seen, and that of their father later that weekend. Their bodies were taken to London for burial.

10 JUNE 1859

It was reported in the *West Briton* that Mr Angove died near Scorrier Gate, and as he was in a club at the time, it was customary for some of the surviving members to carry the body and attend the funeral in a respectable manner. This was clearly not the case on this occasion; the bearers had been too determined to give him a jolly send-off, and were very drunk. They behaved in a 'disgraceful manner, sometimes running at full speed' and leaving the other mourners and singers far behind, using profane language, and threatening to drop the body on the high road – which they eventually did. Some of Angove's relatives lost patience and decided to convey his body themselves to the final resting place in a more respectful fashion.

11 JUNE 1904

Chas Hoad shot himself at his home in South Street, St Austell. He was still alive when found, but died of his injuries soon afterwards. For some years he had been manager for Mr Broad's branch drapery establishment at Redruth. Although well known and very popular in the neighbourhood, he was said to have been worried and much depressed by business problems. He left a widow and young son.

12 JUNE 1941

Barbara Linton (9), daughter of Francis Linton of Plymouth, died in Helston Cottage Hospital after a kick from a horse on the farm of Mr and Mrs John Reed of Melrose, Mawgan-in-Meneage, where the child was billeted. Her mother, also called Barbara, said her daughter had settled down well at the farm. Joyce McCarthy told the inquest that she, little Barbara and another evacuee went to go on the pond at Melrose Farm to collect tadpoles. Barbara suggested that they should go across the field, and to do so they had to climb over some barbed wire. They saw a horse and several cows in the field. They had not played in the field before, but they had often seen the horse on previous occasions in the farmyard. Barbara went up to the horse, telling the others it would not hurt her. She started to smooth down its hind quarters. It kicked her and knocked her down. She got up, then walked a short distance and fell, tried to get up again but was unable to do so. She was taken to hospital, but died from shock and haemorrhage, and a post-mortem examination revealed a ruptured liver.

13 JUNE 1897

Mrs C. Tavener was charged at Launceston Magistrates' Court with obtaining 1s from J.H. Cory, a butcher, by falsely representing that she was a canvasser for the United Christian Mission for Fallen and Outcast Women, Kennington Road, London. Sergeant Parkyn traced her to Okehampton and then Holsworthy, where he arrested her. She had given several addresses of people in London when out canvassing, some of which turned out on investigation to be correct. The court asked for her to be remanded until 15 June, and bail was fixed at £5.

14 JUNE 1865

The Condurrow Mine at Camborne was the scene of a serious accident. Two brothers, named Treloar, were working in the back at a level of 230 fathoms, on a good course of tin, when several tons of material fell away, knocked down the stage on which they were working, and nearly filling in the level in which two other miners John and William Roberts, also brothers, were working at the time. All were buried in the resulting debris. Both the Treloars were pulled out, but had suffered serious injuries. The body of John Roberts was not found, and the rescue party thought it would probably take at least two or three days to find him because of the mass of matter that had fallen. A son of one of the Treloar brothers was working on another stage, and as soon as danger struck, he impulsively threw his hands out in front of him. As luck would have it, he saved himself by coming into contact with a piece of timber in the side of the level, and holding onto it firmly until he could be rescued.

15 JUNE 1937

Philip Davis (30) went on trial at Bodmin, charged with the murder of his wife Wilhelmina (33) and their niece Monica Rowe (15) at their home at Tuckingmill, Hayle. Monica had recently moved in with her aunt and uncle, whose marriage had been in trouble for some time. Davis, a turner and fitter at the local engineering works, who had a history of mental instability going back to childhood, was losing patience with his wife, who tended to lie in bed most of the day while he was out working. She was probably suffering from depression after they had lost two children in infancy in quick succession.

When his wife and niece disappeared in April 1937 Davis told family and friends that they had gone away and left him, taking a lot of his money with them. Neighbours and police had their doubts and suspected otherwise. He rented a garage from his landlord, Mr Andrew, and later that same day he was seen moving barrow-loads of soil and stones inside. The landlord was convinced all was not well. After a friend helped him make a thorough search of the premises, they traced a hideous smell to the inspection pit, and found human remains. They contacted the police, who confirmed that the bodies were those of the missing women.

When he was arrested Davis confessed to having killed them, saying, 'I done the both of them in with a hammer,' adding that he had a row with his wife the night before he went to work. Later he explained, 'I have been in a mental home and I suppose I must be out of my mind.' A post-mortem revealed that Monica was not a virgin, and it was believed that he might have been caught in *flagrante* by his wife with the girl, struck his wife with a hammer, and then had to eliminate his hysterical niece in order to prevent her from informing on him. His defence of insanity during childhood failed to move the jury, who were out for thirty-five minutes before delivering a verdict of guilty. He was hanged at Exeter Gaol by Thomas Pierrepoint on 27 July.

The pit in the garage at Pendarves Street, Tuckingmill, where the bodies of Wilhelmina and Monica Rowe were discovered. (© Devon & Cornwall Constabulary)

16 JUNE 1884

A fire alarm was raised at Falmouth when several people passing by noticed flames coming from the bedroom window of the house occupied by Mrs Best, proprietor of a woollen and fancy business in Killigrew Street. People formed a human chain passing buckets of water, and the fire was soon extinguished. It was found that somebody had left a gas lamp burning in the bedroom, and when the window was opened, a wooden blind was blown near it and set alight.

17 JUNE 1901

Valeri Giovanni (31), an Italian sailor, went on trial for murder at Bodmin. Late the previous year he had come on board Liverpool-based ship *Loxton* at New South Wales, setting sail for Falmouth on 7 December 1900. The only Italian on board, and unable to speak a word of English, he came into conflict with Victor Balieff, a cook by profession, who had come aboard at Durban. Balieff took to teasing him and other members of the crew joined in, but Balieff was apparently the one most responsible. Giovanni accused him of threatening him, and on 15 February he stole a knife from the cook's quarters, went for Balieff and stabbed him through the heart. He was immediately arrested and kept in irons until the ship docked at Falmouth in April, where he was then taken into custody.

On 17 June he went on trial at Bodmin. He pleaded guilty, although on the advice of his counsel he then withdrew it and entered one of not guilty instead. In his defence it was claimed that Balieff had made numerous threats against Giovanni, including one to put him in a bag and throw him overboard. Nevertheless, in his summing up the judge remarked that it had been such a vicious assault that it was difficult to suppose one man could inflict such injuries on another without intending to kill him. The jury returned a verdict of wilful murder, with a recommendation to mercy. While in the cells awaiting his fate, Giouanni made a full confession of his crime to a visiting clergyman. He was hanged at Bodmin Gaol by James and William Billington on 9 July.

18 JUNE 1862

Dr Felce of Launceston went out for a drive in the town on this date with his wife and two female companions. As they were returning home about 9 p.m., half a mile from the town on Tavistock Road, their horse suddenly became restive. They alighted from the carriage, allowed the animal to calm down, and got back in again. When they entered the town, the carriage overturned and all four of them were thrown into the road. Dr Felce was the most seriously hurt, sustaining a fractured thigh and other smaller injuries. His wife had one eye injured and multiple bruising, but the others were unharmed.

19 JUNE 1911

Mr W. Smith, a plumber, was clearing a pipe supplying a public convenience in Camelford during a storm when a coil of wire he was using was struck by lightning. Smith was lifted off the ground and badly injured.

20 JUNE 1956

Eight youths from Birmingham pleaded guilty at Liskeard Magistrates' Court to maliciously damaging an ancient stone figure of a winged griffin which held a metal lance with a metal pennant. It belonged to George Bray, an antiques dealer at Polperro, and was normally cemented to a 4ft-high gatepost in his garden. Pieces were found on the ground after its disappearance was reported. One of the men, Douglas Connop, said they had removed it earlier in the year and taken it in turns to carry the figure back to their car and placed it in the boot, but intended to return it at Whitsun. Their defending solicitor explained that they had done so in a fit of 'youthful exuberance'. Mr Metcalfe, the Chairman of the Magistrates, said that they realised the escapade was due to exuberance 'and possibly to the evening you had spent beforehand, but you have given the police and other people quite an amount of trouble.' They were given a conditional discharge for twelve months and ordered to pay £18 0s 7d costs to cover damage.

21 JUNE 1882

Nicholas Lyne (50), of Tregouse Farm, Mawgan, was returning home with a friend, Mr Williams, after inspecting some cattle in a field. Suddenly he complained that he was feeling unwell and could not stand. With help he was moved near a hedge where he could sit down, and a message was sent to fetch assistance. The surgeon, Mr Haswell, appeared as soon as he could, and Lyne was taken to Tregarrick House, but was dead by the time they arrived there. He had been well known in the district for his exhibits of prize sheep and horses at local agricultural shows, and on the previous day he had taken several prizes at the St Keverne Show.

22 JUNE 1913

Frederick Crowle (40), assistant manager of the Cornwall Electric Power Company, Hayle, died from his injuries in Redruth Hospital after an accident. He had been riding his motorcycle down East Hill, Tuckingmill, on the previous day and was thrown off the vehicle when its wheels struck the kerb. His head hit the pavement, and he also collided with a passing miner, whose leg was cut open.

23 JUNE 1871

Joseph Barrett (53), a customs collector at Penzance, was travelling on a train from Penzance to Truro. According to the Chacewater and two female witnesses, while the train was crossing the viaduct near Truro, Barrett opened the door of the second-class compartment where he was travelling alone, at about 12.30 p.m., and jump from the carriage step over the viaduct. Falling a distance of nearly 100ft, he was dead by the time his mangled body was recovered. As he fell, he had struck one of the timber supports of the viaduct before plunging to the ground, covered with piles of rocks and rubble from a disued quarry. He landed spreadeagled on his back. His injuries included cuts on the back of his head and face, a broken left leg and right arm, and bones could be seen protruding through his clothing.

A childless widower, he had been in poor health for some time, suffering from congestion of the lungs. In November 1870 he had been granted six months' sick leave on full pay. Having tried to resume work about three weeks earlier, he found himself unable to do so, and the Board of Customs gave him a further month's leave on half pay. He was in the habit of going to stay with his brother and family at Truro. This time he was meant to be accompanied by his cousin Miss Harris, who was acting as his nurse, but he dissuaded her at the last moment. As he boarded the 11 a.m. train at Penzance, those who noticed him said he seemed to be dreading the journey by rail.

An inquest into his death was held that same evening. His superior, Alexander Philips, examining officer of the port of Penzance, confirmed that he had known the deceased for over fifteen years, said he had suffered from mental depression, and on the morning of his death had said in despair that he would never be fit for duty again. A verdict of suicide while suffering from temporary insanity was returned.

24 JUNE 1788

A party of thirty-three men and boys and four women went out in a fishing boat at Port Levett, near Helston. The vessel capsized and there were no survivors.

25 JUNE: Midsummer Customs and Superstitions

It is said in Cornwall that if a young unmarried woman stands at midnight on Midsummer's Eve in the porch of the parish church, she will see passing in front of her in procession everyone who will die in the parish during the coming year. Needless to say, few women have been brave enough to dare try the experiment. Stories have been told of those who have, and have seen shadows of themselves. From that day onwards they have pined, and before midsummer comes around again they have been laid to rest in the village graveyard.

Less forbidding superstitions in Cornwall relating to this day say that if a young woman takes off the shift which she has been wearing, washes it, turns it inside out, and hangs it across the back of a chair, then waits until midnight, the man she will marry will appear and turn the garment over. Another says that if a young lady walks backwards into the garden on this day and picks a rose, she will find out who is to become her husband. The rose must be sewn up in a paper bag, and put aside in a dark drawer until Christmas Day. On Christmas morning it must be opened in silence, and the rose must be pinned to the garment on her breast, so she can wear it to church. A young man will either ask her if he can take the rose, or else take it without asking, and he will be the man she will marry.

It was also said that all Cornish witches regarded Trews, near Zennor, as their home. On Midsummer Eve they would light fires on the nearby granite dolmens, or prehistoric chamber tombs, in the hills, then assemble there to renew their vows with the Prince of Darkness. The precise spot where they gathered was marked by a large pile of granite blocks, called

Zennor, close to the area regarded by Cornish witches as their home.

the Witches' Rock. To touch it was thought to be a safeguard against bad luck, though it has since been removed.

26 JUNE 1671

Hugh Acland, one of the main diarists of Stuart Cornwall, recorded that Peter Pollard broke into a house at St Columb where there were two young women, one a relative of his, the other a servant. The latter was lying in bed sick at the time. He seized his relative, struck her in the head with a hammer and left her for dead, then went for the servant and cut her throat. Meanwhile his first victim had come round, and on seeing what was happening, tried to stop him from attacking the other woman. However, he was too strong for them, killed both, helped himself to £150 in silver and £60 in gold, then set fire to the house and ran away. The alarm was soon raised by other people in the town, and when he returned home his neighbours noticed that there was blood on his clothes. He was arrested on suspicion of double murder and denied it at first, but then made a full confession, and was gaoled at Launceston. A similar penalty awaited his mother and father, whom Acland called 'Consenters in this Horrid Act', as they were found to have encouraged him to commit the crimes.

A plaque on Blackheath Common, south east London, in Delabole slate, commemorating the Cornish rebellion of 1497, inscribed in Cornish and English.

27 JUNE 1497

Michael Joseph (Michael An Gof) and Thomas Flamank were hanged, drawn and quartered at Tyburn and their heads displayed on pikestaffs on London Bridge. They had been the leaders of a Cornish rebellion against the new taxes Henry VII was levying to finance an invasion of Scotland. Joseph led a march to London, beginning at St Keverne and joining Flamank and his supporters at Bodmin, but their untrained and poorly-armed force of about 8,000 was no match for the King's superior force which surrounded them and fought a pitched battle at Deptford Bridge on 17 June. At least 300 men were killed and Flamank was captured. An Gof fled, but was soon captured at Greenwich. Both were condemned to death a week later in the White Hall at Westminster. Just before their execution, An Gof said he would have 'a name perpetual and a fame permanent and immortal,' while Thomas Flamank remarked, 'Speak the truth and only then can you be free of your chains.'

Over the centuries 27 June has been celebrated as An Gof Day, with annual events in Bodmin, St Keverne, and London dedicated to their memory.

On the eastern side of the Norman tower of Redruth Church are two grotesque gargoyles representing Henry VII and his Queen, Elizabeth of York. The headgear on the male figure is very like that in portraits of the king, and they were apparently created and erected as Cornwall's response to the suppression of the rebellion.

28 JUNE 1906

Thomas Casley (76), a retired miner who lived at St Just, was found dead, hanging from a beam in the kitchen of his cottage.

St Just. (© Dr Neil Clifton)

Royal Cornwall Infirmary, Truro.

29 JUNE 1862

Mr Stevens, a farmer at Chacewater, was driving a wagon fully laden with hay. He was sitting on the shaft of his vehicle and while turning a corner one of its wheels fell into a rut, and he was shaken off the seat into the road. He escaped the fore wheel, but the hind wheel passed over him, and he was taken to Royal Cornwall Infirmary where he died from internal injuries.

30 JUNE 1872

William Pascoe, a sawyer, was charged at Helston Quarter Sessions with felony. Returning to his house at Helston while drunk, he threatened to burn the place down. Ordering his wife to take their child out of the cradle, he then set fire to the straw in the bed. Then he went upstairs, brought down another child, and handed it to his wife. Next he placed the cradle and its burning contents near the stairs, but before it could do any damage, it was taken outside and the fire soon extinguished. Two constables arrived and took him into custody. The recorder, Mr Prideaux, told the jury that not only a determined intent, but also reckless or indifferent causing of fire would be sufficient to convict. A verdict of not guilty was returned by the jury. In conclusion, Mr Prideaux told the prisoner that he had had a narrow escape. The evidence would have justified the jury arriving at a different verdict, in which case he would have had to pass a severe sentence. A plea of drunkenness was no extenuation, and he warned the prisoner 'against indulging in that deadly sin'.

JULY

Truro Cathedral, the scene of a building accident on 8 July 1908.

1 JULY 1864

A notice in the *West Briton* reported that:

> This is to give notice that I, James Cooke, of Falmouth, in the county of Cornwall, builder, in consequence of the gross misconduct of my wife, Ellen Cooke, have determined from this date to live separate and apart from her, and have made her a separate weekly allowance sufficient for her support, and that, from this date, I will not be responsible for any Debts she may contract. James Cooke.

2 JULY 1824

The servant of Mrs Mitchell, who lived at Launceston, was worried when her mistress did not appear for breakfast as usual one morning. She went up to her room and found Mrs Mitchell lying near the chimney. Going closer to look, she saw that Mrs Mitchell was dead, having managed to strangle herself by tying her garters round her back and to a nail in the chimneypiece, just over 3ft from the floor. She was evidently so determined to do away with herself that she must have continued to press with nearly her whole force on the garters round her neck until she was no longer capable of rescuing herself. As she had been in comfortable circumstances, and was not known to have any financial worries, the inquest returned a verdict of insanity.

3 JULY 1838

The Revd Charles Neet was travelling from Penzance to St Ives for a church missionary meeting. At about 5 p.m., near Halsetown, the horse he was driving took fright, and he and his servant were both thrown from the gig. The servant was unhurt, but Neet fell on his head and suffered several major injuries, including a fractured skull. A St Ives clergyman, the Revd Havart, arrived with medical assistance, but nothing could be done; Neet was already unconscious and remained in a coma until he died at 1.30 a.m. the next morning, leaving a widow and one young son. The horse ran into the town, but did not cause any damage.

4 JULY 1958

John and Daphne Oldfield, both aged 33, were on honeymoon at a small hotel in Bude. They lived in Surrey, where he worked as an insurance clerk, and had arrived in Cornwall on 28 June by train after their wedding at Thames Ditton earlier in the day. This evening they went to a dance and Daphne spoke to a few young men while they were there, apparently provoking bitter jealousy from John. Afterwards they went for a walk together along Maer Cliff, behind the hotel. At a point about half a mile along, the path approached a steep vertical drop onto a pebbled beach about 120ft below, and John took this opportunity to give his wife a sharp nudge, pushing her over. Although she fell some distance, she was only slightly hurt. He caught up with her, hit her over the head with a large stone, then took off his tie and tried to strangle her. Walking away, he left her for dead, but after a telephone call was made to Bude police station just after midnight, she was found still alive and fully conscious by a constable on Crooklets Beach at about 1.30 a.m., and taken to Stratton Hospital.

She had severe multiple injuries, and the hospital staff thought that only the relatively thick clothing she was wearing at the time had cushioned the blows and saved her life. Meanwhile her husband, who had returned to the hotel and taken an overdose of Carbromal, was found unconscious in the bedroom and also moved to Stratton Hospital. After regaining consciousness, he was charged with attempted murder but made no effort to reply. He later appeared at Bodmin Assizes, was found unfit to plead on the grounds of diminished responsibility, and died shortly afterwards in a criminal mental hospital.

5 JULY 1946

At a meeting of the Saltash British and Foreign Bible Society the Revd J. Perry-Gore, rector of St Dominick, spoke of the enthusiasm he had seen among the West Indian population for reading the Bible. A family Bible was to be found in almost every house, worn and well-used, however, Perry-Gore said, 'My experience in England has not been the same. Usually the Bible is not worn as the result of being used, but of being not used – from dry rot, damp and dust.' Mr Symons, the Baptist church secretary, said that it was by reading the Bible and the application of its teachings, rather than by meetings of foreign ministers and security councils, that peace would be achieved.

6 JULY 1898

Stephen Carn, the Penzance borough overseer and rate collector, was reported missing. He had last been seen in Exeter on Sunday 3 July, but since then had not returned home. At a meeting of the overseers, they decided there was no course open for them but to apply for a warrant for his apprehension. They decided to call a meeting of the Penzance Guardians for the following day and ask them to declare the office of collector vacant, thus giving them authority to appoint another. The accounts were found to be in some disarray and had to be unravelled, and it would not be possible for them to say for a while what amount of deficiency there was, if any. Up to £50 was covered by a guarantee society. Nothing was known as the result of an audit, which had taken place on behalf of the Income Tax Commissioners, but it was understood that they had been pressing for payments for some days, and that explanations given them by Mr Carn for not supplying them at once were considered unsatisfactory. Whether it was merely a case of muddled accounts, they could not say. Mr Carn's family had declared themselves willing to make good any deficiency that might arise.

7 JULY 1549

Martin Geoffrey, the parish priest of St Keverne, was executed in London. In 1547 the Book of Common Prayer in English replaced the old liturgical books in Latin, a move which was particularly unpopular in Cornwall, which had long been a bastion of Roman Catholic sympathies.

As part of the Church's campaign against 'popery', in which traditional religious processions and pilgrimages were made illegal, one of the commissioners appointed by Archbishop Cranmer to remove all symbols of Catholicism from churches in England was William Body. When he came to remove and destroy images from Helston parish church in April 1548, a crowd gathered, seized him, dragged him into the streets and stabbed him to

Launceston Castle. (© Phil Wright)

The Prayer Book Memorial, near the site of Glasney College, Penryn. The college was destroyed in 1548.

death. Retribution followed swiftly when twenty-eight Cornishmen who were accused of aiding and abetting were arrested and executed at Launceston Castle. Geoffrey was taken to London and hanged, after which his head was then cut off and impaled on a spike on London Bridge.

8 JULY 1908

An accident occurred during the building of the western towers at Truro Cathedral. The men had been working at a distance of about 70ft from the ground, and just before the dinner hour a lift or cage used to convey materials to the top was sent up. After it had been unloaded a party of six men entered for the purpose of being taken down, as had been normal practice – though a notice saying that they did so at their own risk was attached to the lift. It came to the ground with a crash, and five of the six occupants were injured. They were taken to the Royal Cornwall Infirmary, and three were detained with serious injuries to their thighs and legs. One of them had to have a foot amputated.

Truro Cathedral,
The Nave looking East

9 JULY 1846

A thunderstorm beginning at about 1 p.m. caused a flash flood at East Wheal Rose Mine, near Newlyn. As it was in a natural bowl, the flood waters filled the mine in very little time. A rescue party was soon organised, and 300 people were quickly set to work piling up earth around the collars of the shafts in a brave but ultimately unsuccessful attempt to hold back the accumulated rainwater from pouring down the shafts.

Heavy wind extinguished the miners' candles underground and left them in total darkness. However, one rescue worker managed to climb the slippery ladders down the mine against the weight of water cascading down after him, while Samuel Bassion, a timberman, went into the mine to lie across a manhole and divert part of a flood, thus saving eighteen men. The beam engines were put to work to raise other men to the surface who clung to kibbles and chains, it was said, 'like strings of onions'. By the time rescue operations were more or less completed forty-three men and boys were still missing. Four were found and brought up alive next morning, leaving thirty-nine dead and missing.

An inquest was held at the courthouse of the mine on two of the bodies found, and the jury expressed themselves satisfied that every effort was made in the first place to prevent water from getting into the shafts, and next in trying to preserve the lives of the men still below. The lower levels had been completely flooded, and it took four months to clear all the water and accumulated debris and get East Wheal Rose in full production again.

10 JULY 1946

Harry George Eggins, a butcher of Fore Street, Saltash, pleaded guilty at Callington Magistrates' Court to being in unlawful possession of a spear and gaff for the purpose of taking salmon. On behalf of the Tamar and Plym Fishery Board, Mr J. Barker said that on 10 July a water bailiff saw the defendant crossing the Tamar, and saw both implements lying on the ground. The defendant admitted being the owner, and offered to send a cheque to any local hospital or charity the Fishery Board cared to name if the bailiff agreed to overlook it. This was not accepted, and he was fined £5 and 30s costs.

Fore Street, Saltash. (© Kevin Hale)

Falmouth harbour.

11 JULY 1882

During the afternoon William Gott, a member of the Salvation Army, left Falmouth harbour in his small pleasure yacht. A gale blew up shortly afterwards, and by the time he was about two miles off the Manacles he was overtaken by a fierce squall. His yacht was last seen by another sailor making for a place of safety, but heavy rain fell, and nothing was seen of the yacht afterwards. It was believed that Gott and his vessel had been lost.

12 JULY 1865

The body of Mr W.H. Harvey (21), son of Mrs Sarah Harvey of Tintagel, was found on Trebarwith Sands. He had gone to swim on the previous afternoon,

but was thought to have been seized with a severe attack of cramp while out at sea and was unable to return to shore. Although he lived in London, he had come back to Cornwall the previous week to visit his mother for a few days.

Trebarwith Sands.

13 JULY 1830

Stephen Karkeet (25) was working underground in the mine at Newlyn when the sides of the shaft he was in, five fathoms below the surface, fell in. The first person to arrive at the spot was George Trevarrow, a fellow miner, who called down to ask if anyone was there. Back came Karkeet's voice, 'I know all earthly power can avail me nothing, I feel the cold hand of death upon me; if there is any hope of my being extricated from this untimely grave, tell me; and if not, tell me.' Trevarrow told him that four tons of rubbish had fallen around him, and that there could be little hope. 'All's well,' replied the victim, 'it is the Lord, let Him do what seemeth to be good. Tell my dear father and mother not to be sorry as those without hope for me, 'tis now only that I am happy, 'tis now I feel the advantage of a religious life, now I feel the Lord is my stronghold, and now I feel I am going to heaven.' At this point his voice failed him.

14 JULY 1929

Annie Langdon, of Lumar Row, Truro, had spent the last few days on holiday at Mousehole with Mrs Alice Hall at Cleria House, and was due to return home the next day. She decided to go out in the afternoon for a picnic lunch with Mrs Hall's daughter and Lottie Dyer, and they walked along the top of the cliffs. The path ran very close to the edge, and Miss Langdon warned her friends to take care and watch they did not slip. A few minutes later she herself suddenly stumbled and fell forward over the edge of the cliff onto the rocks about 20ft below. Miss Hall and Miss Dyer both shouted for help. Philip Worth from Mousehole came to help, climbed down the cliffs to where Miss Langdon was lying, and found her unconscious and badly injured. He took off his vest and tore it into strips to use as bandages, then went for assistance, returning a little later with his father and other friends. They took Miss Langdon in a boat back to the town, where a district nurse and a former naval man rendered first aid. She was moved to West Cornwall District Hospital, Penzance, but died of her injuries soon afterwards.

15 JULY 1820

Henry Polgrean died at his Ludgvan home after having been very sick the previous evening. His wife Sarah (37), who already had one failed marriage behind her, was notoriously unfaithful to him, they frequently quarrelled, and she had been heard by neighbours threatening to poison him. At first it was assumed he had passed away from natural causes, but the gossiping of others soon became too much to ignore and eleven days after he was buried the police gave orders for his body to be exhumed. The contents of his stomach were examined, and it was found that he had consumed a lethal quantity of arsenic. Police enquiries revealed that Sarah had recently purchased some in Penzance, claiming it was to be used for killing rats at home, although the house had never been known to have a problem with vermin. She was arrested and charged with murder.

Her trial was held at Bodmin on 10 August. She protested her innocence, but the evidence against her was overwhelming and she was found guilty. While awaiting execution she made a full confession, admitting that she had mixed the arsenic with a portion of butter and spread it on her husband's bread. She attributed the crime to a lack of religious education and to having been a victim of sexual abuse by a fellow servant during her years in service, when she was no more than a child. She was hanged on 12 August.

16 JULY 1877

Two separate cases of drunkenness were brought before the courts. At Penzance Guildhall, before the county magistrates, Walter Treleaven Boyns, a labourer from Paul, commonly known as 'Skimbo', was fined 10s and costs or two weeks in prison. As he had no money, he received a custodial sentence. Meanwhile W. Warrell, also known as A. Spargo, appeared before the Mayor of Penryn, Mr M. Lavin, for using obscene language at the Swan Inn, Penryn, on 14 July, and threatening to strike the landlady, Mrs Richards. He pleaded ignorance, as he was drunk at the time, and was fined 33s plus costs.

17 JULY 1829

William Ennor was found dead on the cliffs between Lower St Columb Porth and Newquay. He had been shipping a quantity of china clay on board a vessel on the coast, and as he was returning along the road near the cliff, he fell over. It was assumed that he was drunk at the time.

18 JULY 1945

An inquest was opened at Truro by Mr L. Carlyon, county coroner, on the death of a newborn female child, the daughter of Grace Shear from Probus. Dr Hocking said the death was due to suffocation. Dora Childs, the district nurse, said she found Grace sitting at a table in the hospital in tears and her sister had told her, 'Grace has had her baby and I don't know what she's done with it.' The baby's body was later found in a pail of water. Proceedings were adjourned for four weeks awaiting further reports.

19 JULY 1894

Joseph Simms of Falmouth appeared before the town magistrates charged with assaulting his lodger, Mary West Lanyon. After returning home very drunk one night, he had struck Mrs Lanyon in the face, took her by the arm, dragged her to the door, and then let her fall, causing her to injure her back on the doorstep. In his defence, he explained that Mrs Lanyon had been told to leave the premises six months previously, and she had 'cheeked' him, so he took her by the arm to lead her out through the door. A police constable told the Bench that Simms had had a drink problem for some time.

Simms' wife Martha also accused him of having threatened her, and both parties had last been in court a few weeks previously. Mrs Simms claimed she had been threatened forty times, and found it very difficult to obtain money from her husband for day-to-day expenses. The mayor, Mr T. Webber, described them as an ill-matched pair, and said he could quite understand that if Mrs Simms's tongue went at the same rate at home as in the court, it must be very tantalising for the husband – at which point laughter was heard. It was evident that Mr Simms did not want to have Mrs Lanyon living on his premises any more, and the mayor urged Mrs Simms to co-operate with her husband in inducing the lodger to leave. Simms was fined 10s and 11s costs, and was bound over to keep the peace for six months.

20 JULY 1909

William Hampton (23) had the dubious distinction of being the last person ever hanged at Bodmin Gaol. During the previous year he had become engaged to Emily Tredrea, then aged 15, and moved in to her family home at Vicarage Row, St Erth. However, she was increasingly irritated by his persistent swearing and other uncouth habits, and at length realised that she no longer cared for him. She told a friend in the village that she feared and hated him, and was anxious that if they stayed together he might kill her.

On 1 May 1909 she told William that it was all over between them, and that she was breaking off their engagement. He hoped she would change her mind, but when she repeated herself the following evening he lost his temper, grabbed her and throttled her with his bare hands. Leaving her body propped up in a chair, he ran out of the house in the direction of Hayle. Emily's younger brother William and mother quickly alerted the community to what had happened, but there was no need for them to mount a search as the killer gave himself up to the police at about midnight. 'I was going with her, and now she won't have anything to do with me,' he said as he confessed to his crime. 'I suppose it was temper that made me do it.'

*Bodmin Gaol. (©
Kim Van der Kiste)*

He went on trial at Bodmin on 24 June 1909, and in summing up the evidence the judge, Mr Justice Phillimore, said that the act had not been a momentary one. It appeared that the prisoner had intended for some time to take the life of the deceased. The jury took fifteen minutes to find him guilty, but with a recommendation to mercy, which proved to be of no avail.

21 JULY 1930

At Falmouth Police Court, Joseph Cantania, a Maltese sailor, pleaded guilty to being drunk and disorderly on regatta night and assaulting Constable Tamblyn. The latter said that the prisoner was in the centre of a large crowd in Market Street that night, using profane language and behaving in a manner likely to cause a breach of the peace. When asked to go quietly he refused, and had to be taken into custody. While being taken to the police station, he became very violent, struggled with the constable and bit him on the fingers. At the time he had £14 5s 6d on his person. As he was about to join a ship, the Chairman of the Bench said he would deal leniently with him, fining him £1 for being drunk, and £3 on the charge of assault.

22 JULY 1871

John Annear, a miner at Redruth, was injured at Pednandrea Mine, when his shirt sleeve was caught in a wheel while he was greasing the rods. He was removed to the accident ward of the Miners' Convalescent Hospital at Redruth, but in a very weak state.

23 JULY 1957

An inquest was held on the death of Jessie Godson (46), of Fore Street, St Ives, by the county coroner, Mr P.J. Chellew. She was the wife of Frank Edwin Godson, a bookseller, and the previous evening, when he went upstairs after finishing the day's work in his shop, he had discovered her dead body in the bedroom with a rifle by her side. He said her nerves had been getting increasingly bad since April, but she had seen a specialist and was waiting to undergo treatment for depression. The weapon had been in his possession for a good many years, and he had never imagined that she would use it on herself.

24 JULY 1912

George Green (33), a postman, and Archibald Goldsworthy (20), a hairdresser, both of Redruth, appeared before Bodmin Assizes. They were charged with conspiracy to try and obtain £8 11s by a forged postal packet from a bookmaker at Plymouth, and Green was also charged with trying to obtain £11 5s by a forged postal packet with intent to defraud. Both pleaded guilty and were sentenced to three months' imprisonment.

25 JULY 1929

A detached garage in a field at Halfway House near Wendron was burnt out early in the morning. It was the property of Gordon Albert Truscott, who lived half a mile away. The Penryn Fire Brigade was summoned, but by the time they arrived the garage had been completely destroyed.

Penryn.

26 JULY 1893

At Torpoint Petty Sessions, Christopher Nicholls of Kingsand was fined 2s 6d and costs for assaulting Philip Phillips. William Richards, of Trematon, was fined 10s and costs for inciting his dog to worry a lamb. For stealing apples at Antony, four boys, James Worth, Albert Gilbert, William Bradley and George Ferris, were each fined 7s 6d including costs. Private Taylor, KOSB, was fined 10s plus costs for being drunk and disorderly. Lance-Corporals Tom Stamp and Charles Cooper, of the same regiment, were dismissed on similar offences after paying costs.

27 JULY 1878

Selina Wadge (28) went on trial at Bodmin Assizes, charged with murdering her two-year-old handicapped son Harry by throwing him down a well in a field near Launceston. At the time she was engaged to a labourer, James Westwood. When she was asked by her family what had happened to Harry, she said first of all that he had died from a throat disease. After being questioned further she changed her story, saying that Mr Westwood had taken the boy from her and killed him, then threatened to do the same with the elder boy, five-year-old Johnny, but she ran away from him in time to stop him from carrying out his threat. Later she broke down and admitted having killed the little boy herself. Her motive for doing so was that Westwood had agreed to marry her on condition that she got rid of the boy.

At the trial at Bodmin he denied having said any such thing. He said he had always been fond of both of her sons, and was perfectly prepared to be a good stepfather to them after he was married. She was convicted of murder, but a recommendation of mercy was made because of her 'previous love for her children'. While awaiting her execution, she confessed to the murder and 'admitted the justice of her sentence.' She was hanged by William Marwood at Bodmin Gaol on 15 August.

28 JULY 1935

A large family party left Barnstaple in three cars for an outing at Stanbury Mouth, eight miles from Bude. They went bathing after luncheon, and shortly afterwards six members of the party were seen by others on the beach to be in difficulties. Inspector Prout of Stratton appealed to all boat owners in the vicinity to put to sea and try to recover the body of William Baron, which had been seen floating in the breakers. The sea was very rough and they were unable to do so. Two others, Mrs Emily Palmer and Mr Barker, were drowned, and their bodies were taken to Bude mortuary.

29 JULY 1886

At lunchtime James Hawke had two glasses of beer at the Navy Inn, Penzance, and then went out for a short cruise in the harbour with the landlord and another friend. On his return he went to see some other friends and chatted to them as normal. Without any warning he suddenly left and came back a few minutes later, telling them abruptly that if they did not 'clear out from here I will soon settle the lot of you.' He then produced a gun, and shot dead three of the company, Mr and Mrs Uren, and Mrs Gerrard.

A neighbour of the Urens, Rebecca Roberts, heard a sound which she initially thought sounded like boys letting off crackers in the lane. She saw a body lying in the yard, went to her front door, noticed Hawke and asked him what he was doing. He took a purse from his trousers and a watch from his waistcoat pocket, asked her if she would give them to Mr Uren's daughter, then shook hands with her and said goodbye to her 'as coolly as if he had been going on a journey.' He then put the weapon to his head and shot himself.

At an inquest at the Penzance Guildhall on the following morning, none of the witnesses said they had previously noticed anything peculiar about his behaviour until he embarked on his fatal rampage. Nobody could offer any reason as to why a man who had seemed his normal self just minutes before, and none the worse for drink, despite visiting the inn, should suddenly take the lives of three people and then his own.

30 JULY 1850

An inquest was held in Illogan on William Nettell (15), who had drowned the previous day while bathing in the engine pool at North Pool Mine. Several boys were looking on at the time, but the water in the pool, except round the edges where the deceased and other boys had been bathing, was 6ft deep, and they were all afraid to go in after him. The first man who arrived at the spot did what he could to save him, but as he was unable to swim he had to give up. Shortly afterwards one of the dressers, John Harris, went in and recovered the body, which was taken into the engine house, where every effort was made to resuscitate him but in vain.

31 JULY: Cornish Witchcraft Trials

During the seventeenth century, about a dozen witch trials were held at Launceston. One of the towers at Launceston Tower is known as the Witch's Tower because of a belief that witches were burnt at its base, though under English law all those convicted of witchcraft were usually hanged.

In July 1686 Jane Nicholas was accused of bewitching John Tonken, aged about 15, and tormenting him. It was claimed that she appeared before him, sometimes in human form, 'at other times like a Cat; whereupon the boy would shriek, and cry out that he could not see her, laying his hands over his Eyes and Mouth, and would say with a loud voice, she is putting things into my Mouth, she will choke me, she will poison me.' In later visions she appeared in the shape of a mouse, and left through the window, but would never give him her name. She told him he would not be well until he had vomited nutshells, pins and nails. He brought up straws, rushes, pins, brambles, needles and nails, but his tormentor always appeared beforehand to warn him whenever he was going to vomit. She was charged and put on trial but found not guilty.

AUGUST

The Charlotte Dymond memorial, erected on Rough Tor near the scene of her murder, for which Matthew Weeks was executed on 12 August 1844. (© Nicola Sly)

1 AUGUST 1945

Thomas Henry Trebilcock (35), a farmer of Trebarber Colan, was charged with triple murder at a bungalow near Newquay. His alleged victims were Mabel Georgina Tonkin (57), a housekeeper employed at the bungalow; Edith Legge (56), wife of a nearby farmer; and Kathleen Owen, Mrs Legge's two-year-old grandchild.

Trebilcock, it was said, had 'got religion', and it had entered his disordered mind that most people were sinful beyond redemption and did not deserve to live. Miss Tonkin was found in the kitchen with her head and face battered in, lying in a pool of blood surrounded by fragments of skull bone and brain. A broken vacuum cleaner nearby, stained with blood to which were adhering strands of her hair, was evidently the 'blunt instrument' with which she had been beaten. Mrs Legg had also been battered, with a piece of wood found near her body, and the child had met with a similar fate. Trebilcock was said to have been in the habit of asking people if they were, or had ever been, wicked. If they answered yes, he considered they were not fit to live, so he despatched them. He entered a plea of not guilty to murder and was committed for trial at Bodmin Assizes.

2 AUGUST 1898

Among the passengers on the 9.45 a.m. train from Penzance on the West Cornwall branch of the Great Western Railway was Mrs Taylor, a young mother with her child in her arms. She was the wife of an employee of Andrew Lawrey, a market gardener of Ludgvan, and this was only the second time she had travelled by train. She was going to Marazion, the first station, but instead of alighting while the train was in the station she retained her seat. As she explained afterwards, she had been expecting that somebody would open the door of the compartment for her. The train, which was driven by two engines, had left the station and was proceeding at a speed of about 15mph, when a quarter of a mile from Marazion station she was seen to unfasten the handle of the door, and with the child in her arms leap from the footboard of the train onto the side of the permanent way. The train immediately pulled up, and the guard went to the assistance of the woman, who was found to be in a serious condition, although her child was unhurt.

The pulling up of the train had attracted the attention of officials at Marazion station, who also proceeded up the line and took charge of Mrs Taylor and the child. Mother and child were taken to the stationmaster's house adjoining the station, and every possible attention was paid by the railway authorities. Dr Mudge was sent for, and he found that the woman was suffering from slight concussion and internal injuries. He said she would be certain to recover after a period of rest as long as she was taken straight home.

3 AUGUST 1894

Frederick Keast was charged at Callington Petty Sessions with moving two pigs without a licence on 22 and 23 July, in contravention of an order issued by the Executive Committee of the local Sanitary Authority of the County of Cornwall. The defendant did not appear, but had asked Pensilva Constable Jarrell to inform the Bench that he admitted the offence, pleading that it was committed in ignorance of the law. He was fined £2 and costs. The chairman, Mr Digby Collins, said a good deal of money was being spent by the government in an effort to stamp out swine fever, and that it was the duty of everyone to acquaint himself with and conform to orders issued on the subject. The defendant had rendered himself liable to a penalty of £20.

4 AUGUST 1865

Mary Richards, a shellfish saleswoman, was charged at Helston Court with stealing a piece of pork worth 3s from the Duke's Head Inn nearby. Mrs Copus, the landlady, said she saw the prisoner in her back kitchen, and when she went to look for the pork a few minutes later it was missing. On going to look for Mrs Richards, she found her in another inn, with the meat in her pocket. When charged, the prisoner said it was 'the fault of the liquor' she had been drinking. Although she had no previous convictions, she was sentenced to two months' imprisonment with hard labour.

5 AUGUST 1882

Mr Waite, on holiday at Brunswick House, St Ives, was walking along the cliffs at Porthminster Hill when he missed his footing and fell onto the rocks below. A doctor examined him and found that he had broken two ribs as well as injured his spine.

Porthminster Hill.

6 AUGUST 1839

John Martin, Samuel Hayden, George Bastian and John Tripconey were all indicted at Bodmin Crown Court before Mr Justice Coleridge for 'having violently assaulted, molested, hindered and obstructed' Francis Beatty and Philip Calf, two boatmen working for HM Customs, employed to prevent smuggling at St Keverne. The jury acquitted Tripconey, but the others were found guilty and sentenced to twelve months' hard labour, the first and last week to be served in solitary confinement.

7 AUGUST 1862

An inquest was held at Fowey Cottage Hospital on John Jago (50), who had been killed the previous day after a cannon suddenly exploded. A widower who lived with his wife's stepdaughter, he had been attending Fowey Regatta and was asked to fire the gun for starting races. He was not used to artillery and the cannon which he had been placed in charge of had not been properly examined. When he fired it, it burst near the muzzle. A piece of iron from the gun struck him above the ear and he was killed at once, the top of his head being blown away and his brains scattered. The jury returned a verdict of accidental death.

8 AUGUST 1937

Two young men and a young woman, all from Camborne, were drowned at Hayle Bar, about three miles from St Ives. They had gone for a bathe at midday, but there was a strong current running and soon they were in difficulties. An alarm was raised and the ferry boat put out, but it capsized in the strong current, though the captain managed to get ashore safely. A motor boat also put out, and two of the crew managed to pick up the woman, but she was already dead. Dragging operations were continued in the hope of recovering the other two bodies.

9 AUGUST 1839

Shortly after 6 p.m. the driver of a horse-drawn cart in Falmouth came to Thomas Michell's house to borrow a quill so he could blow some salt into the eyes of one of his horses, which he had accidentally struck with a whip. Michell had no quills in his house, so he sent for one. It was believed that he knew what the quill was really required for, and that he had previously supplied the same driver with one on another occasion. Both men went to the cart, bored a hole in a barrel of spirits in the cart, and began to suck the contents through the quill. Two or three other carts which were passing at the time were halted at the same spot, and each of the drivers joined the first two men. Michell did not appear to be the worse for drink, but admitted he had had a drop or two of brandy from one of the carts which had just moved off. He did not wake the next morning, so a surgeon was sent for but found it impossible to arouse him. By the afternoon he was dead from the effects of having consumed too much raw spirit.

10 AUGUST 1861

Several men were working in Penryn slate quarry. They had been driving rock wedges, or iron bars, into a slit of one of the rocks to break it up and make it easier to deal with, but finding that this was unlikely to work, they decided instead to throw it down when their other workmates were at breakfast and therefore out of danger. However, the mass of stone gave way without warning and fell. One block, which was estimated to weigh about 5 tons, struck a man, who was killed instantly. Such was the force of the rock that, 'his heart was found entire, about five yards from the body, and when seen first actually palpitated.' One of his arms was also completely severed and thrown some distance from the body. Three men who were suspended by ropes had a narrow escape. Fragments of rock were hanging over their heads, and had the ropes been cut by falling rock, they would almost certainly have perished as well.

11 AUGUST 1813

An inquest was held at Morvah on the body of a young woman, aged about 25, who had visited a druggist at Penzance to purchase arsenic on the pretext of wanting to poison rats. As she was 'a person of respectable appearance' she had no difficulty in obtaining some from a chemist. Back at home she told her mother that she had been out to get some powders for a pain in her stomach, and immediately poured the arsenic into a cup of tea, which she promptly drank. A few minutes later she began to retch badly, and continued to do so for the next four hours, until she expired in agony.

At a post-mortem her stomach was found to be greatly inflamed, and the presence of arsenic left no doubt as to the cause of her death. It was also discovered that she had been carrying twins of about six months' growth. The jury returned a verdict of *felo de se*, and the next day she was buried, in accordance with the usual custom for suicides, at a crossroads where four different parishes met.

12 AUGUST 1844

Matthew Weeks was hanged at Bodmin Gaol for the murder of Charlotte Dymond. Both had been in service at Penhale Farm, near Davidstow. They began walking out together, but it all went wrong for Matthew when an old workmate of his from the past, Thomas Prout, suddenly appeared and threatened to steal Charlotte's affections. On 14 April she tried to get away for a secret rendezvous, presumably with Thomas, and she did not return. Spots of blood were later found on the sleeve of Matthew's coat, and a search was carried out on Rough Tor, on the edge of Bodmin Moor. Her body was found lying partly submerged in the stream; her throat had been slashed from ear to ear.

At his trial Matthew confessed that they had gone for a walk and he had accused her of disgraceful behaviour with another man. She had turned her back on him, retorting that she would do as she pleased, at which he lost his temper and lunged at her with a pocket knife. He thought he had come to his senses and put the weapon away without harming her, but when she repeated her remarks he lashed out again and injured her fatally. Panic-stricken by the sight of her body falling on the ground with blood pouring from her neck, he hid her clothes and discarded the knife as he ran away. He was arrested and went on trial at Bodmin for murder, and his execution was witnessed by a crowd of nearly 20,000 spectators. A granite monument was later erected in Charlotte's memory on Rough Tor, close to the scene of the murder.

13 AUGUST 1936

William Foxcroft (18), from Preston, on holiday with his parents at the Edgcumbe Hotel, Newquay, was at the scene of an incident on a cliff bounding the Barrowfield. He had tried to scale the cliffs, and reached a point where he could not go up or down. His plight was first noticed by Mr Reynolds, a taxi proprietor from Newquay, who drove to the coastguard station and reported the matter. Two coastguards, Mr Warman and Mr Puddifoot, borrowed a taxi for their gear and drove to the cliff top. They found the cliff was perpendicular and in a badly crumbling state. The gear was brought into action and Coastguard Warman was lowered down to the boy down the

Charlotte Dymond's grave, St David's Church, Davidstow. (© Nicola Sly)

200ft cliff. He found the boy in a very nervous state, and had some difficulty in persuading him to put on the cliff rescue apparatus. The boy then agreed to be rescued, and the coastguard experienced more difficulty, as the boy could not assist himself and almost had to be carried to the top. By now a crowd of about 500 visitors had congregated along the railings to see what was to them a novel experience. At the cliff top, several more coastguards were ready to help. It was agreed that the boy was lucky not to have been killed.

14 AUGUST 1909

A young man at Heamoor was alleged to have tried to murder Elizabeth Nicholson (22), who worked for a firm of newsagents. He had lately been paying attention to her, and while they were together that night screams were heard. Elizabeth was subsequently found with severe wounds in her throat and neck. She was taken to her home, where she was in a critical condition for some time. Her suitor was later discovered in a garden, also with wounds to the throat. There was evidence that he had also jumped into a pond in order to try and drown himself, but without success.

15 AUGUST 1867

At the Truro Board of Guardians, the Revd J. Perry brought to their notice the case of a woman with five children, living in the parish of Perranzambuloe. About three years previously her husband had died, leaving her with four children unprovided for, and until about two months previously she had been in receipt of 6s a week from the Union. At that time she gave birth to an illegitimate child, upon which the relief was stopped, and she was offered the workhouse. She refused to enter the workhouse and instead went out every day to work, leaving her children locked up in a room without any furniture, and with one shawl as the only article of clothing among them. The eldest of her family was eight years old. They were regularly left without any food all day unless the neighbours, who were very poor themselves, took pity on them and offered them some. The Guardians decided that the woman should again be 'offered the house', and if she refused it she should be brought before the magistrates on a charge of cruelty to her children.

16 AUGUST 1834

The family of Mr Henwood, in the parish of Liskeard, were horrified to discover two pieces of wax candle next to a rick of wheat, deposited in such a manner as to leave no doubt that they were deliberately placed there in order to set fire to the stack. The ends of both pieces were placed inward, almost in a horizontal position. Judging from the appearance of the wicks, it seemed that both had been lighted, but were extinguished by the overflow of wax, after having burnt for a very short period. Whoever had done it had probably hoped that the farm and outhouses, being mostly covered with thatch, would catch fire as well. The position of the candles suggested that the party responsible would have given him, her or themselves adequate time to escape before the fire could be discovered.

17 AUGUST 1865

At a crowded Falmouth Guildhall James Murray, captain of the *British Crown*, of Liverpool, was charged with ill-treating one of his crew. Local solicitors were engaged for both parties. David McMillan gave evidence that while at sea on 9 July, the starboard watch was called to haul the lee clue of the mainsail aft. The clue got foul of one of the rattlings, and he went to clear it, the captain being at the time on the poop; all hands were present. He got three rattlings up when the captain swore at him and ordered him down. As he did so, the captain grabbed him by the hair, kicked him down on the main deck, from a height of about 10ft, and then struck him. The witness told him he would pay for what he had done, to which the captain retorted that he 'would have the worth of his money out of him.' McMillan was then pulled under the break of the poop by his hair, severely beaten about the face, and put in irons. When the cook remonstrated with the captain, he was also put in irons. The witness was then ordered on the poop, and as he was going there the captain knocked him over the spar. As he was getting up the captain kicked him again, then went to breakfast, and afterwards ordered the boatswain to get two earrings, or pieces of rope about 15ft long. One was made fast to the iron between the witness's hands, and the end thrown over the spanker boom, and made fast to a belaying pin in the rail. As the ship was rolling, the boom was swinging backwards and forwards. McMillan was swung off the deck for three or four minutes, and the boatswain came and lowered him until his toes touched the deck, leaving him in this position for half an hour. The captain then called the boatswain, saying, 'Let that fellow down; he has got enough of it.' Two or three witnesses were called for the defence, but the magistrates thought the case was sufficiently serious to be sent for trial at the next county sessions.

18 AUGUST 1862

John Doidge (28) was hanged at Bodmin Gaol for the murder of Roger Drew (57) at St Stephen-by-Launceston on 7 June. Drew's wife was in service, and he lived alone, trading as a grocer and carpenter. It was commonly supposed that he kept a large amount of money in his house. On 8 June Mary Martin went to buy something from his shop, found the shutter had not been put up, and the door locked. Looking through the window, she saw him lying on his face on the floor in a pool of blood, and noticed that the tables and chairs had been moved around as if the premises had been burgled.

Doidge, a labourer who lodged opposite, had recently been out of work, and was starving. His landlord Mr Sutton had ceased to supply him with food, and threatened to turn him out. Drew and Doidge both frequented the same public house, the Smith's Arms nearby. On the previous evening they were seen in friendly conversation together. Doidge was seen by Mrs Sutton early on the following morning with a large billhook which he used for cutting wood, trying to conceal it behind a water barrel. It was noticed that he had spots of blood on his coat, shirt and trousers, which he had worn on Saturday night.

When Drew's house was examined by police, it was found that a cash box in his bedroom had been broken into. There were bloodstains on the stairs and in the bedroom, and it was thought that Drew had been attacked while getting ready for bed that night, as he had a slipper on one foot and an unlaced boot on the other. A post-mortem found that the blow on his head was so severe that death must have been instantaneous. Doidge, who had been suspected of setting fire to a house in the village two years previously, was immediately taken into custody on suspicion of murder, charged at Bodmin Assizes on 6 August before Mr Justice Williams, and found guilty.

19 AUGUST 1880

It was reported that an inquest had been held at Falmouth the previous day on the death of Michael Kelly (42), who died suddenly on board the passenger steamer *Lady Wodehouse*, bound from London and Southampton for Dublin. He had served in the army for over twenty years, and was discharged from the 20th Regiment at Cyprus on 24 June. The discharge was confirmed on 14 August at Netley, and he was on his way to Dublin where he intended to settle down. A verdict of 'died by the visitation of God' was returned.

20 AUGUST 1864

The *West Briton* reported that Calstock was 'unhappily being visited by an uncommon degree of mortality.' The Revd F.T. Batchelor, the local rector, had just lost his infant son, the third son of his to die within the last seven weeks. A miner recently buried his four daughters, while several other families in the district had had to endure the sudden loss of two children or more. Another miner, Mr Allen, lost three of his daughters the previous Saturday. Only a week earlier all had been in excellent health, and the eldest, aged 14, had just received her pay after working at the local mine.

During the month of July sixteen children had been buried, and in August there were twenty-five funerals, while there had been more than 150 deaths in the parish during the year so far, out of a population of 7,500. The epidemic had been exacerbated by the intense summer heat and a corresponding shortage of water. As the deaths had been occasioned by malignant fever, the rector had very properly refused to allow bodies to be taken into the parish church, fearing that otherwise infection might spread among the congregation.

21 AUGUST 1901

Henry Thomas Mortimer, aged about 42, murdered his wife Georgina (33), their young children Eric, Alan, Madge and Kennedy, and then himself at their house in Saltash. At about 3.15 a.m. their neighbours Charles Palmer and his wife heard the sound of gunshots, and when nobody emerged from the house during the day, they feared the worst. The police entered the building later that night and found the fully dressed body of Mortimer in the front bedroom, a double-barrelled gun between his legs, the muzzle pointing towards his head, his head shot away. His wife was in the bed, and at each side of the bed was a cot with a child in each. All had also been shot in the head, with much of their faces blown away.

At the inquest held on 22–23 August, it was stated that Mortimer, a native of Watford, Hertfordshire, was not married to Georgina, as he was previously married and his first wife was living elsewhere. He was considered 'an excitable man, and 'of loose character', yet temperate in his habits, and although 'of uncertain temper' he had always been apparently on good terms with his 'wife' and fond of his children. Only a few days earlier he had told Mr Palmer that he was planning to move to Southampton. At the time he was playing with his children and seemed to be perfectly happy. He was considered of sound intellect, but to have profound religious views which made him think that he ought to do away with his family. While devoted to the children, he apparently feared that they might have 'inherited his own tendencies to evil', so he decided that all of them would have to die.

22 AUGUST 1941

An inquest was held at Camborne into the death of Godfrey Spittle (13), who drowned off the coast there the previous day. His father Richard had warned him not to go into the sea as he could not swim. Nevertheless, he took a fishing line and swimming costume with him. The sea was very rough that day and his father saw him treading in deep water, crying for help. He tried to reach the boy, but the latter had already been swept out to sea.

23 AUGUST 1919

Mrs Ernest Pollard, a fisherman's wife, died at St Ives whilst trying to rescue her husband from a burning building. Mr Pollard (36) had been invalided out of the Royal Navy during the war, and had since become paralysed and blind. After she had lit an oil lamp in the kitchen of their cottage, she took their two children out to play on the beach, leaving her husband in bed in a room on the third storey.

On her return, she found the kitchen on fire and the flames spreading rapidly. She did her best to check the fire, and then rushed upstairs to her husband. She managed to lift him out of bed and get him to the front window, but before anyone could get a ladder both husband and wife fell backwards and disappeared. The building, mainly of wood, burnt so quickly that all hope of rescue soon had to be abandoned, and when the fire died down their two bodies were found resting on a ledge inside the window. She was still clasping her husband and leaning over as if to try and shield him from harm. The cottage was completely burnt out, and there was some damage to an adjoining house. The basement of the cottage had been used as a grocery store.

24 AUGUST 1853

The body of a child aged six months, buried a month earlier, was exhumed as there were grounds to believe it had been murdered. The child and its father, Mr Pellow, a miner who lived at Metherell, near Harrowbarrow, were taken ill with food poisoning, and although the father soon recovered, his infant died. When Mrs Pellow and William Tregay, their lodger, both suddenly disappeared, foul play was suspected and the deputy coroner, Mr Hamlyn, was alerted. He ordered the child's body to be disinterred.

An inquest was held, and it was proved by witnesses that Tregay had procured poison for Mrs Pellow on several occasions. She had eloped with Tregay immediately after the child's death, and she had already tried to kill her husband by putting poison in a pasty she had prepared for him which he took to the mine when he went to work. He ate some and was violently sick, drank some warm salt and water and vomited up the rest. A dog belonging to a fellow miner had gobbled up the rest of it and died almost at once.

The enquiry was adjourned to await the evidence of Mr Jones, who established the presence of arsenic in the child's stomach sufficient to cause the deaths of three adults. A verdict of wilful murder was returned against Mrs Pellow, and later that week she and Tregay were arrested at a lodging house in St Austell.

25 AUGUST 1887

Francesco Poggi, an Italian member of the crew of the brig *Sant Antonio*, was due to be charged with murdering chief mate Enrico Ciampa on board ship.

The vessel had docked in Falmouth harbour on 19 August and a quarrel between both men, which had simmered during the journey, boiled over into a fight. Initially it was with bare fists, but then Poggi attacked Ciampa with a sheath knife, slashing into the jugular vein on his neck, and cutting the left-hand side of his face. Ciampa was given immediate first aid and doctors were called to see him, but he had bled to death by the time they arrived.

Claiming that he had acted in self-defence, Poggi was restrained by the ship's crew members, and arrested. When he appeared before the town's magistrates next morning, he demanded the services of an interpreter from Italy, and promised that when he was brought before a proper tribunal, he would reveal exactly what had happened. He was examined by two doctors, who considered that he was insane and unfit to plead. The case was adjourned, andPoggi was sent to Broadmoor while arrangements were made to hand him over to the Italian government.

27 AUGUST 1662

A group of Quakers were arrested while meeting at Nicholas Jose's house in Launceston. Including Jose himself, nine men and five women were taken into custody and appeared before Justice Godolphin at the next assizes. Four of the men were each fined 40s and held in prison for five years, while the rest were committed until they could find sureties for their good behaviour and imprisoned for nearly two years. The Quakers' leader, George Fox, and two friends had spent nine miserable weeks in Launceston Gaol in 1656, and Fox described the experience in graphic detail:

> The place was so noisome that it was observed few that went in did ever come out again in health. There was no house of office in it; and the excrement of the prisoners that from time to time had been put there had not been carried out (as we were told) for many years. So that it was all like mire, and in some places to the tops of the shoes in water and urine; and he would not let us cleanse it, nor suffer us to have beds or straw to lie on. At night some friendly people of the town brought us a candle and a little straw; and we burned a little of our straw to take away the stink. The thieves lay over our heads, and the head jailer in a room by them, over our heads also. It seems the smoke went up into the room where the jailer lay; which put him into such a rage that he took the pots of excrement from the thieves and poured them through a hole upon our heads, till we were so bespattered that we could not touch ourselves nor one another. And the stink increased upon us; so that what with stink, and what with smoke, we were almost choked and smothered. We had the stink under our feet before, but now we had it on our heads and backs also; and he having quenched our straw with the filth he poured down, had made a great smother in the place. Moreover, he railed at us most hideously, calling us hatchet-faced dogs, and such strange names as

Above: *George Fox, the Quakers'
leader, who was among those
imprisoned in the dungeons at
Launceston Castle.*

Left: *The Launceston Castle
dungeons, surmounted by a plaque.
(© Phil Wright)*

The plaque recording the Quakers' imprisonment. (© Phil Wright)

we had never heard of. In this manner we were obliged to stand all night, for we could not sit down, the place was so full of filthy excrement.

28 AUGUST 1929

William Sprackling (19) of Falmouth pleaded guilty at East Kerrier Petty Sessions, Penryn, to stealing a silver watch valued at £2 2s from a man's coat in a field at Budock. Superintendent Nicholls said that Sprackling had several previous convictions. His father, Albert, was charged with receiving the watch and paying 2s for it. When asked how his son got the watch, he said his grandmother gave it to him. William was bound over for twelve months, as the chairman said they were prepared to give him one more chance. His father claimed that he had no idea the watch was stolen. He was bound over for six months in the sum of £5 and ordered to pay costs of 19s.

29 AUGUST 1856

A notice was published in the *West Briton*:

> I hereby give notice that my son Joseph Coulson Thomas, about 35 years of age, now residing in Camborne, has been for some time incapable of doing any business, owing to a complaint in his head, and I caution people against doing any money transactions, or supplying him with any Intoxicating Liquors. (Signed) John Thomas. (Witness) James Rule.

30 AUGUST 1863

The down train on the West Cornwall Railway ran off the line at Penweathers Junction, about a mile from Truro. The driver was killed, the stoker severely shaken, and the breaksman suffered severe scalding. The accident had been caused by a trolley being placed on the line by person or persons unknown. The engine, tender, and three carriages broke through the bridge and fell over into the road.

31 AUGUST 1887

Mrs Crowther, a widow who had settled at Mannamead, Plymouth, was staying at Downderry for a few days with her family of ten children. In the morning she, eight of her children, and a domestic servant, went to bathe at Seaton Beach. The seas were very rough at the time, and Mrs Crowther was the first to come out of the water. While she was dressing

Shag Rock, Seaton Beach.

A MOTHER SEES HER THREE DAUGHTERS DROWNED AT DOWNDERRY, CORNWALL.

Mrs Crowther trying in vain to rescue her three daughters from drowning at Seaton Beach in 1887. (Penny Illustrated Paper and Illustrated Times)

126

afterwards she heard some of her daughters screaming. To her horror she saw that the waves had carried three, Julia (23), Florence (18), and Jane (12), some distance away from shore. It was thought that one of them had been carried out by the waves, so the others had gone to her rescue, and all were struggling hard to get back to safety. Rushing into the water, Mrs Crowther tried to reach out to them, but failed and narrowly avoided being swept away and drowned herself.

She shouted for help, and sent one of her other daughters and the servant to get assistance. Brian Williams, an army captain who was helping the coastguard at the time, swam to her through the ever-worsening seas. At some risk to his own life he managed to get her ashore, by which time she was exhausted. A doctor was sent for, she was given restoratives, and soon recovered sufficiently to walk back to her lodgings. Tragically, the girls were not so fortunate. Boats were sent out to search for them, but during the afternoon only Julia was recovered. Attempts to resuscitate her were made for over two hours, but in vain. Florence's body was found two days later, and that of Jane was washed ashore on 15 September.

Mrs Crowther was the sister of Thomas Lea, Liberal Unionist Member of Parliament for South Londonderry from 1886 to 1900. It was her second family tragedy on the same beach, for her husband had died from the effects of sunstroke after bathing there seven years previously.

SEPTEMBER

Mylor Creek, where Henry Nicholls killed himself on 21 September 1866.

1 SEPTEMBER 1875

At Callington Petty Sessions, two small sons of a local builder were charged with damaging a well at Pengelly and fouling the water in it. William (7) and Alfred (5) Irwin were found playing at the well on 11 August, had broken the boards 'and a nuisance had been committed in the water'. The Bench found both boys guilty, and fined them £1 plus costs. At first the father said that as the children were in Court and not him, the Bench could send them to prison in lieu of the fine. They were removed to the police station and kept there until 9 p.m., when their father, 'repenting of his determination not to interfere in the matter', changed his mind and paid the fine plus costs of £2 8s.

2 SEPTEMBER 1644

The end of the Civil War in the South West came with a battle fought near Lostwithiel. It was in effect a campaign which concluded with the surrender of the Parliamentary force in Cornwall. The previous month, King Charles had marched west in pursuit of a Parliamentarian force under the command of the Earl of Essex, who in July had invaded the county. Although it was a Royalist stronghold, Essex had been persuaded that his presence in Cornwall would be able to rally a certain amount of support for Cromwell. Having reached Bodmin, he found the people as Royalist as ever, and decided to withdraw to Lostwithiel. Once the king and his men arrived there were several small clashes between both forces.

At the end of August the Parliamentarian infantry were driven back towards Fowey in pouring rain, and had to abandon much of their artillery which was bogged down in muddy roads. On 2 September Sir Philip Skippon, the Parliamentary Sergeant Major General of Foot, was left in command while Essex commandeered a fishing boat and escaped to Plymouth, abandoning the 6,000-strong infantry and artillery. Skippon wanted to

Sir Philip Skippon, leader of the Parliamentary forces at the Battle of Lostwithiel in 1644.

Bodmin, where the Earl of Essex arrived shortly before the Battle of Lostwithiel.

fight, but his officers and men knew it was a lost cause, and he surrendered on this day.

The king was keen to conclude the campaign before enemy reinforcements could arrive, so he granted very generous terms. The defeated army was allowed to surrender its artillery, weapons and stores, and retreat on the condition it did not take up arms again until it reached the Parliamentary garrisons at Portsmouth or Southampton. As the disarmed and dispirited troops marched out of Lostwithiel in pouring rain, they were ambushed and attacked by local men who claimed they were merely recovering their own plundered property. About one thousand soldiers died of hunger, exposure or disease, and another thousand deserted.

3 SEPTEMBER 1880

A fire early in the morning destroyed the paper mills belonging to Messrs Mead at Penryn, and seriously damaged the surrounding property. The mill and stock were valued at over £30,000. Two firemen from Falmouth fell from a roof into the fire but were rescued and made a good recovery from their injuries.

4 SEPTEMBER 1934

An inquest at Redruth under Coroner Barrie Bennetts returned a verdict of accidental death on Hugh Brown Gerrard (48), of Liverpool, who had died at the house of his brother-in-law, Dr G. O'Donnell, of Clinton Road, Redruth, on the previous day. In November 1933, while working at Battersea Power Station, Gerrard, an electrical engineer, was pulling a chain and injured his left hand. A temporary dressing was applied, and next day he was treated at St Thomas Hospital, London. He came to stay with Dr O'Donnell on 8 December, intending to remain there for the weekend, but was so unwell he stayed in bed on his brother-in-law's advice, and remained under medical treatment

Penryn, where a fire destroyed a paper mill.

there until his death. Dr MacDonald attributed death to septicaemia as a result of the hand injury.

5 SEPTEMBER 1820

Michael Stephens was executed at Bodmin after being convicted at the assizes in August for sheep-stealing. Immediately after his sentence he hoped that mercy would be shown him and that his death sentence would be commuted, but as he was about to attend a sermon being preached in the prison chapel on the morning of the execution of Sarah Polgrean (*see* 15 August), he was informed that this would not be the case. Before going to the gallows he admitted that it was a just punishment, and he attributed his fate 'to the loss of his character, on having, on a former conviction, been imprisoned for a year; the effect of which was his being hardened in guilt, and fitted for the perpetration of further offences.'

6 SEPTEMBER 1863

At about 8.30 in the evening, the warehouse of Richard Stevens, cabinet maker and builder at Kenwyn Street, Truro, caught fire. In less than two hours his warehouses, workshops, and furniture rooms, together with their contents, and those of the adjacent timber yard, 60 sq. yds in total, were destroyed.

131

Mr Stevens was the owner of the property, which was about 350ft in length, with an average width of 60ft. He had ordered a wagon-load of straw for mattresses which should have been delivered during daylight, but arrived much later. As he had to leave for a prior appointment, he asked one of his workmen living nearby to take in the straw, showing him where it was to be placed, on the ground floor of the western warehouse. The delivery men who came with the wagon stored the straw by candlelight, and then left at about 8 p.m.

Mr Stevens returned home half an hour later, and a few minutes after that his servant girl ran in to raise the alarm. He went out to check, and found the warerooms and workshops in flames. A large crowd of people gathered, and engines were sent at once to Kenwyn Street. The larger one was at first placed in Mr Martin's coal yard, nearly opposite Mr Stevens's premises, but as the supply of water there was inadequate, it was moved to the corner of Castle Street, and fed by means of a suction hose from a reservoir supplied from the leat by the gutter in Edward Street. This also proved insufficient to control the flames, and from then on they had to rely on water from a supply of buckets. The fire-fighters were helped by some heavy showers of rain, and by 10 p.m. the fire was extinguished well enough to forestall any fears that it might extend further.

Afterwards Mr Stevens estimated his total losses at £600, of which his insurance would cover about £450. The warehouse upstairs was full of finished furniture, doors, window panes, partitions and similar articles for a job which he had in progress, while the ground floor of the building was filled with timber, prepared flooring, dry wainscot, paints, oils and a nearly new morticing machine. All the workmen's tools, valued at about £50 and uninsured, were also destroyed.

7 SEPTEMBER 1909

The body of Helen Lewis (60), of Apsley Villas, Clapham, London, was discovered floating off the Pentire side of Fistral Beach. It was thought that

Fistral Beach, Newquay.

she must have gone too near the edge of the cliff while she was watching the breakers and lost her footing. At an inquest at Newquay the jury returned a verdict of 'found drowned', but saw no reason to believe that she had intended to take her own life.

8 SEPTEMBER: Port Quin

The fishing village of Port Quin, about two miles from Port Isaac, is known as the Cornish 'village that died'. One night, probably in the early years of the nineteenth century, the total population suddenly disappeared. Several different theories have been offered. It was thought that the village may have been smitten by a sudden epidemic, after which the survivors buried their dead and dispersed elsewhere, before news of the illness had a chance to spread and result in them being ostracised by those in neighbouring communities.

Another possibility was that a ship got into difficulties on the rocks near the end of the inlet into the village during a heavy gale, and that all the local men who tried to help in the rescue were lost together with their boats.

Other theories have it that the village had been heavily dependent on the proceeds of smuggling at the end of the eighteenth century, and somebody had received due warning that a raid by Customs & Excise could be expected very soon, so everybody fled before the long arm of the law could catch up with them; or that the entire male population were drowned one particularly stormy night while they were out fishing, and as the women could not continue to live there on their own, they decided to go elsewhere.

The most credible, and generally accepted explanation, was that the herring and pilchard fishing on which the village depended gradually declined, the local mines closed down, and people simply moved away.

Nevertheless it was said that when the last survivors departed, they not only left food on the tables, but also went with the rooms still furnished, and made no effort to take their clothes or other personal possessions with them. It was as if every family had been summoned outside for a temporary evacuation or fire drill and expected they would return within minutes, but for some reason never did.

Port Quin. (© Tony Atkin)

9 SEPTEMBER 1889

Joseph Matthews, of Lostwithiel, was kicked by a horse in the head and fractured his skull. Dr Bennett was soon in attendance, and the boy recovered.

10 SEPTEMBER 1911

Edward Atkinson (72) and Bevil Quiller-Couch, who was many years younger, went on the River Fowey for a midnight sail. Their boat, about 16ft long, had two sails and was protected by two bulkheads, which were supposed to be airtight. Although it was fairly old, it had been kept in good condition, and was thought to be perfectly safe. During the summer it had been moored in the river. Soon after they started the wind blew up from the east, and at midnight they anchored under Pencarrow Head, staying there until 10 a.m. the next morning when they started for Fowey, two and a half miles away. By then the wind, which had been very strong, had calmed down to some extent. However, a strong gust of wind struck the boat on the beam, and the well of the boat filled with water. The bulkhead also became flooded, and the boat dipped at the stern. Quiller-Couch heard the air rushing out of the bow bulkhead, and he and Mr Atkinson decided that it was best to leave the boat at once, as she was drifting to leeward, where the sea was rougher. They were about 400yds from shore. Mr Atkinson was fully clothed and could swim, but he was not very strong and was affected by the shock of the boat going down. Quiller-Couch pulled him towards the shore, but the steep rocks were standing clean out of the water at that point and there was no beach. The wind was against them, and although they got within 10yds of the shore, the backwash of the waves meant that Quiller-Couch could not pull the by now exhausted Atkinson in. The latter motioned for him to go ashore and get help. Quiller-Couch climbed the rocks and cycled to Polruan. The coastguard and a pilot stopped a tug and went out to help, while Quiller-Couch cycled back to the cliff, but by this time Atkinson was dead.

A verdict of 'accidental death' was returned. Quiller-Couch said he thought the bulkheads of the boat gave way through the wood being cracked while the boat was lying in harbour. The jury expressed sympathy with Atkinson's family, and appreciation of the conduct of Quiller-Couch, who had done everything possible to save his companion.

11 SEPTEMBER 1829

A severe coastal gale was felt particularly in the Padstow area. In the morning the wind varied from south-east to north-east, but around noon it changed to north-north-west and developed into a hurricane. Several ships were affected; the *Francis* from Torquay capsized while trying to enter Padstow harbour, with the loss of all hands. The *Hector* from Sunderland, with a cargo of iron bound from Cardiff for Ipswich, was driven on shore near Pentire Glaze, and several similar vessels at sea at the time suffered some damage, though no further fatalities were reported.

12 SEPTEMBER 1838

Mr Howarde, keeper of Treleaven Gate, near Penryn, was summoned for detaining John Boeden on the night of 20 August for fifteen minutes at the turnpike gate without good reason. It was proved that he had been negligent in his duty by locking the gate early and going to bed. He was fined 1s 6d and 18s 6d costs.

13 SEPTEMBER 1922

The body of Fred Goolden (51), an architect, was found floating in the sea off the coast at Falmouth. He had gone out Pollack fishing a day or two previously, promising his family he would be back within a couple of hours. When he failed to return, a search party was sent out for him and his boat was found moored by a fishing line which had become entangled in the bottom of the vessel. His body was caught in the line.

14 SEPTEMBER 1839

One of the steam boilers of the works of the Consuls Mine, near Truro, blew up, tearing down the walls of the engine house, and completely unroofing it. James Eady, one of the captains of the mining operations, knowing that several carters had gone into the engine room to dry themselves, went as soon as possible to the spot, but could not see anything, because the connecting pipes to the other boilers had been severed by the explosion and steam was escaping, filling the place. Soon he heard a groan, and with assistance succeeded in removing a large piece of the boiler, under which they found a man named Rickard, who died as soon as they cut his clothes from him. They then took out a Mr Burrowes, who was also dead, as was a Mr Penherrick lying near him, and John Grime. Of those outside the house, Mr Absalom Richards had his head literally blown off from his body; James Truran (16) was badly scalded, and was in a coma, as were two other men who were, however, thought more likely to recover.

An inquest was held the next day on the bodies of the victims, and the engineer gave evidence that the water was at its proper gauge in the boilers, which he had examined only quarter of an hour before the accident. The captain of the mine and the overseers gave the engineer a good character reference for steadiness of conduct. In the course of the evidence it was stated that in the full force of the explosion the top of the boiler was carried to a distance of more than a hundred yards, fell on a cottage, and crushed it, while the wall of the engine house 'was thrown fifty yards off.' A verdict of accidental death was returned.

15 SEPTEMBER 1893

Mr G. White, a Launceston solicitor, and his clerk, Mr W. Cory, were being driven to Stratton Court when their horse was frightened at Langdon by a goat which jumped on the hedge. The horse shied and began to plunge. Mr White, who had been seated behind, jumped off. The horse bolted down an incline, and at the bottom tried to jump a deep gutter. In doing so it threw Mr Cory and Mr Sharrock, the driver, of Launceston Posting Company, out on to the road. Mr Cory sustained injury to his back and severe bruising. The driver was also much shaken and bruised. Mr Shepherd of Launceston was sent for, and went to the scene of the accident. Mr Cory and the driver were brought home in a closed carriage. The vehicle was badly damaged, but the horse was more or less unharmed. The court did not sit until the afternoon as Mr Leigh, the barrister, was thrown out of his carriage at Dolsdon, while on his way to Stratton, in a separate accident.

16 SEPTEMBER 1934

Phyllis Herrold (4), from Southall, fell into the floating dock at Penzance, between the trinity steamer *Mermaid* and the wall. Frank Rose, of Melrose Terrace, Penzance, plunged in fully clothed and brought her to safety.

17 SEPTEMBER 1946

John Tolson Nicholls (75), of Boscaswell Village, Pendeen, fell from a wagon and was killed. Having gone to Carlatha Farm to fetch some milk, Nicholls saw another farmer carrying corn but needing assistance, and went to offer to help. He got onto the wagon and was helping to arrange a load while the wagon was moving towards the rick. As it passed through the gateway, he fell off, went under the wheels and was fatally injured.

18 SEPTEMBER 1948

Trevor Miller (17) of Barnstaple was caught breaking into a house at Kingsand. He was sent by Cornwall Quarter Sessions on 5 October to a

Kingsand.

Borstal institution for two years, and asked for three other offences to be taken into consideration.

19 SEPTEMBER 1922

Yetta Greenburg, a nurse, ran away from her lodgings at Sudbury, Suffolk, and made her way to Cornwall. She was last seen at Chapel Porth, and later an umbrella with her initials was found in the fields between there and St Agnes. A handbag containing a small amount of money and a thermos flask, found on the cliffs, were identified as her property. Before leaving London, she had spoken of suicide, saying it would be a nice death to go to Cornwall, take morphia, lie down on the beach, and let the sea carry her away. Some morphia tablets were found near the spot where she was last seen.

20 SEPTEMBER 1893

Two levels collapsed and eight miners were entombed at the Dolcoath Mine, and several men were injured. It was feared that there was little chance of reaching the trapped miners through the heavy falls of debris and that any left alive would simply starve to death. Some of the men were married, and four of them had families. The lode in which the debris fell was about 30ft wide, and the timberman and a staff of men were securing the ground there when it fell on them with scarcely any warning. Some of those who were saved reached the surface by ladders a mile from the scene of the accident.

21 SEPTEMBER 1866

A report was published into an inquest a few days previously on the body of Henry Nicholls, a former schoolmaster who for the last four years had led a secluded existence. He had purchased a ship's launch which he decked over and converted into a sailing boat in which he lived alone, having no

The Harriet Pumping Engine House at Dolcoath Mine.

communication with the outer world except when he was compelled to go on shore for necessities. During the summer months he cruised about the coast, and in winter he holed up in some creek or other.

The boat was badly damaged during the gales of the winter of 1866 and since then he had remained in Mylor Creek. As he had not been seen on deck for several days, a cousin of his, who lived at Mylor, decided to go on board and check. On entering the cabin he found Nicholls on the bed with his head hanging down on the floor. A revolver pistol was in his hand. He had shot himself in the mouth, and had been dead for several days. The coroner's jury returned a verdict of temporary insanity.

22 SEPTEMBER 1934

William Lake, aged about 35, a hotel employee who formerly lived in London, was arrested in St Ives by Sergeant Osborne and Constable Jones, following information received from Scotland Yard, on a charge of embezzlement regarding a cheque for £108 in 1931, the property of a London firm for whom he used to work as a porter. He had been at St Ives since June 1933 and was employed at the hotel during that time.

23 SEPTEMBER 1941

Ernest Lyons (51), a retired major from the Middlesex Regiment, died at 3 a.m. at the West Cornwall Hospital after a fall from Land's End cliffs on the previous afternoon. An open verdict was recorded at the inquest at Penzance on 25 September by the Deputy Borough Coroner, Barrie Bennetts. Lyons, a bachelor from Cranleigh, Surrey, had been in good health, and was not thought to have any financial worries. He went for a walk in the afternoon to Land's End, and was later found lying between two rocks down the cliff

Land's End.

on the south side of Land's End Hotel. Witnesses telephoned for first aid and an ambulance. He was unconscious when admitted to hospital, and had a fracture to the base of his skull, an incised wound on his chin and bruise on his right hand.

24 SEPTEMBER 1879

Richard Pascoe (50), of St Austell, was charged 'with using a certain inducement' with intent to procure a miscarriage for Edna Chapman of Belowda, Roche, on 10 September, and with administering certain drugs with a similar intent. The case was heard in private. He had a wife and ten children. Known as a quack doctor, he was committed for trial at the next assizes.

25 SEPTEMBER 1871

At Twyardreath Petty Sessions, Susanna Welshman, of the Sailor's Return Inn, Fowey, was charged with assaulting Elizabeth Mallett. The latter had gone into Welshman's brother's house to look for her husband and give him his breakfast, and asked Welshman not to give him any more to drink. The latter insisted on drawing ten pints of beer, threatened to throw Mrs Mallett into the river if she did not leave the house, and smacked her in the face.

Mrs Mallett said that her husband was drunk every day. The Bench fined Welshman 5s with 11s costs. George Mallett was charged with being drunk and disorderly, but did not appear in person. Three months earlier he had been sent to prison for seven days on a similar offence, and this time he was committed again for the same period. A summons against him was heard for non-payment of poor rates, for which he was given a month to pay.

26 SEPTEMBER 1899

Thomas Hart, of Wellington, Somerset, was charged at the Lostwithiel Police Court with hawking umbrellas in public without a pedlar's certificate, and sentenced to seven days' imprisonment in default of a fine of 5s and costs. He was unusually short of funds at the time, as the previous day he had been fined at Twyardreath for having been drunk and disorderly in Fowey on Saturday evening.

27 SEPTEMBER 1943

An inquest was held into the death of Annie Moore Kenner (52), of Manchester, who had been killed on 23 September while on holiday in Cornwall with her husband and son. They were cycling from Higher Alsworthy to Sandymouth, near Bude. Her husband James, a professor of Technology and Chemistry at Manchester University, and son George, were cycling in front of her and were near Frowda Farm, Kilkhampton, when the accident occurred. George told G.L. Andrew, the deputy coroner for North Cornwall, that when he glanced over his shoulder to see if his mother was coming, he saw her riding in the drain on the right-hand side of the road. Her bicycle continued for several yards, and eventually she returned to the road, but seemed to lose her balance, and fell heavily. At no point did she shout or call out for assistance. James said that he was about 100yds in front of his wife and son, and did not see or hear anything. They were experienced cyclists and had been taking such holidays for fifteen years, and his wife's bike had been in perfect condition. Constable Goble said he had found her body on the grass verge, and a wound behind her right ear was bleeding freely. There was no sign of any obstruction in the road. Dr King reported that she had died of a fractured skull.

28 SEPTEMBER 1929

Thomas Mason, of no fixed abode, appeared at Stratton Police Court, pleading guilty to refusing to conform to regulations while he was an inmate of the Poor Law Institution. The master and porter of the institution said

Sandymouth Bay, near Bude, where Annie Moore Kenner died in a cycling accident in 1943. (© James Cosgrave)

he was admitted on the evening of 27 September. After he had created a disturbance in the bathroom and threatened attendants with a table knife, Inspector Pill was telephoned, and took him into custody. He was given one month's imprisonment.

29 SEPTEMBER 1892

Harry Neal (7), of Treveighan, near Camelford, was with another boy three years older, and they went to Tredarrup, a farm near the village. There they asked John Richards (9), a farm labourer, to show them a gun which was kept loaded in the stable. Richards took the gun from the manger and showed it to them. As he did so he accidentally pulled the trigger, and fired a bullet, killing Neal instantly. Richards carried his body home, and explained that he had been putting the gun back in the manger when it accidentally went off.

30 SEPTEMBER: The Extinction of the Willmott Family

In 1600 the Willmott family bought a house at Bolhelland, near St Gluvias, built on a site where it was said bad luck always came to those who lived or stayed there. Three years later the son of the house left home to become a pirate and after several years had made his fortune. He returned home in 1618, but was horrified to see their once proud house now neglected and decaying. Dodging a line of creditors in the drive, he went to the back door, where his sister did not recognise him until he showed her a childhood scar which she remembered well. They decided that for a joke she would introduce him to their parents as a traveller and friend of their son who had come asking for a room for the night, and then went to tell her husband about it.

The son stayed at the house, telling his unsuspecting mother (who had also failed to realize who he was) of his exploits, and making no secret of his wealth. It suddenly occurred to her that if she killed this stranger and stole everything he had with him, she could hide his body, sell his valuables and pay off their creditors. The daughter would be told that he had made an early start to go and rejoin his ship at Falmouth. She then woke her husband, who had gone to bed, and they killed him.

When their daughter returned next morning, they told her he had left. She said she had not thought he would leave so soon – as the scar he showed her proved he was their long-lost son. Mr and Mrs Willmott were so overcome with remorse that they ran up to the room where they had left the body, and killed themselves by cutting their throats. When their daughter wondered what they were doing and went to find them, she was so overcome with grief at seeing what had happened that she fell down and died.

The tale is mentioned in a pamphlet in the Bodleian Library, Oxford, *News from Penrin in Cornwall, 1618*. Who from the family, it has been asked, was left to tell the tale – the daughter's sorrowing husband? Was it a genuine event, or the product of somebody's lively imagination? Whatever the truth of the matter, Bolhelland did exist, though it was a ruin by 1620 and demolished in the mid-nineteenth century.

OCTOBER

Commercial Street, Camborne, close to the scene of rioting on 8 October 1873.

1 OCTOBER 1820

The Mayor of Camelford drew attention to 'a practice in the borough, which was at once a great inconvenience to the inhabitants, at large, an outrage to decency and good morals, and a violation of the Sabbath.' Keepers of 'the common bake-houses, who draw the ovens on Sunday, before divine-service is concluded, at the church,' were carrying dishes of meat through the streets before divine service was concluded. Many of the parishioners therefore had to eat their dinners half-cold, 'as the meat was often half-an-hour to an hour from the oven before they were ready to sit down to it.' The Bench of Alderman expressed their strong disapproval of such a 'scandalous practice', and the mayor was formally asked to put the Act of Parliament against violating the Sabbath strictly into force, against any persons who should open an oven or carry meat from a bake house before the conclusion of divine service.

2 OCTOBER 1943

William Thomas Kellow (35), a farmer, and his cousin Dorothy Kellow (31), both single, had both lived at Spittal Farm, St Mabyn, but very unhappily. Around mid-September Dorothy had invited her 15-year-old niece Muriel Worden, who lived at St Teath, to stay. Since then William had tried three times to kill Dorothy. Once he tried to strangle her, but Muriel pushed him off.

On the morning of 2 October Muriel heard Dorothy say, 'No, Tom, I'm certainly not going to,' followed by his reply, 'You've upset me.' Dorothy then screamed for Muriel, who ran downstairs to find them standing in the dairy doorway. He was pointing a gun at Dorothy's stomach. Dorothy tried to get away but he caught her, pushed her into the dairy, and fired at her. Muriel tried to take the gun away but William swore at her, and told her to go and find their neighbour Mr Long. As she went, she heard another shot. The coroner, Mr E.W. Gill, said she was lucky to get out of the house when she did. On a previous occasion, said Muriel, he had knocked down a lodger at the farm.

St Mabyn.

Kellow's brother, another William Kellow, said there had previously been trouble. He and a local constable had both advised Dorothy to leave Spittal Farm. She had gone away from the farm for a while, but had later returned.

Albert Cox of St Mabyn said Kellow had been to his house on 1 October to borrow a gun, as a fox was stealing his chickens. He lent him a gun and two cartridges. Sergeant Lovering said he found the dead bodies of a man and a woman in the dairy, with a 12-bore sporting gun between them. In the gun's trigger guard was the bent end of an iron poker, and two discharged cartridges. The coroner told the jury he was astonished that Dorothy had a chance to leave Kellow but still returned. 'If she had been in fear of her life before, you would think she would have welcomed the chance of dissociating herself from him.' A verdict of murder and suicide was returned.

The jury foreman, Mr C.H. Paul, chairman of Wadebridge Borough Council, said Muriel had been very brave, and the jurors would very much like to pass her on the fees they would be receiving in respect of their expenses as a result of their duties in court if she would have them.

3 OCTOBER 1931

The *Western Morning News* reported on an extraordinary number of thresher or fox sharks in the Wolf fishing grounds off Land's End. They took a large number of pilchards, though there was no serious damage to fishermen's nets. The thresher shark was known for its long and powerful tail. According to the nineteenth-century Cornish naturalist John Couch, 'the lashing of its tail has been known to put to hasty flight a herd of dolphins.' They have long been common off the county's coast, with several taken every year by fishermen.

More recently, in November 2007 a fisherman trawling for squid and John Dory off Land's End caught a 16ft (5m) shark weighing 1,250lb (568kg), almost twice the weight of the previous largest known specimen caught off Hawaii two years earlier.

4 OCTOBER 1924

May Johns (10) was killed and fourteen others injured after a coach overturned at Camborne. The party was going from Troon to Camborne Market, and when turning a dangerous corner on an incline in Mount Pleasant Road, at the entrance to the town, the coach turned over on its side. The passengers were thrown into the road, and the injured were extricated with some difficulty from the damaged vehicle. Four doctors and three ambulance cars were quickly in attendance, and the injured were taken to Redruth Hospital, where several were treated for fractured limbs. Mrs Solomon Prior and Gwendoline Eustace were found to have received serious injuries.

5 OCTOBER 1879

Mr Phillips, a farmer of Polmarnham, near Kanescot, St Blazey, and his wife found both their sons, aged 3½ and 2½, dead at dinner time. While playing they had strayed into the farmyard and pulled a heavy cart down on themselves, and when they were discovered, it was resting on their chests. A surgeon, Mr Pace, tried to resuscitate them but failed.

6 OCTOBER 1903

Writer Charles Lee (1870–1956) was a Londoner by birth, but he moved to Cornwall in 1893 and spent much of his life in various towns and villages in the county. He kept a journal in which he recorded various observations of the world around him, including an entry for this day in which he commented on a Cornish belief that May cats brought vermin into the house. Florence, his maid, confirmed it, telling him that they would bring adders, 'and all manners of creeping things' indoors. August cats, he decided, were just as bad. He once found his kitten Sambo in the dining room, 'foaming at the mouth, and attempting to eat a fine brown slug.'

7 OCTOBER 1863

At a meeting of the Truro Town Commissioners, the newly-elected Board of Commissioners asked the surveyor about a public well or pump in Rosewin Lane, Pydar Street. It had been used by the poorer population for some years and recently it had been omitting such a dreadful stench that workmen currently employed in the area could not bear to stand anywhere near. The well was found to contain a large quantity of decomposed wood from the decayed pump tree and other sources, and a common sewer opened into it. The poor people of Truro had to place their trust in these public pumps for a supply of water for culinary purposes, and as they were few and far between, the effect upon the health of the neighbourhood by the use of water in such a filthy condition was incalculable. Complaints had already been made respecting the pump two years earlier, and the grievance had only recently been remedied.

8 OCTOBER 1873

Two men were arrested, a new contingent of police was summoned from Bodmin, and several special constables were sworn in after a riot which broke out in Camborne the previous day. Animosity against the police for summoning two miners who had tried to rescue a prisoner led to the disturbance. Several thousand miners, most of them armed with sticks and stones, gathered to try and prevent the prisoners from being taken to jail. Their attempt was frustrated by the removal of the men via a back way by road instead of rail. The rioters then vented their wrath on the neighbouring buildings. The windows of the Magistrates' Hall, the Assembly Rooms and the police station were smashed, while the windows of several other houses and hotels were also attacked. Every time a policeman was seen, there were groans and derisive cheers, and each time another one came into the street he was soon forced to seek shelter in the building.

Several warrants were issued for the arrest of rioters, but many had absconded. When two miners were apprehended and brought before the Bench, witnesses testified to the police having acted with unnecessary violence. Only the presence of soldiers proved as a restraint to acts of violence, and some residents were quitting the area as they feared further outrage. The magistrates issued an order for all public houses to be closed from 5 p.m. until 7 a.m. next day. This, however, was not enough to prevent some of the mob from getting into a number of the houses, particularly Newming's Hotel, where they gutted the premises, took the beer and spirits into the street, drank some of them and poured the rest down the gutters.

Over the next three days the agitation gradually died down, and several miners were arrested for causing a disturbance.

9 OCTOBER 1934

Two members of the British Union of Fascists tried to hold a meeting at the Wharf, St Ives, in the evening. A crowd of 300 gathered and refused to give them a hearing. A couple of Blackshirts were in charge of the meeting, and when one of them denounced all other political parties in strong terms and this was much resented by the audience. There were continuous interruptions, and a threatening attitude was adopted by some members of the audience towards the speakers. Constable Pearn calmed down the crowd who were attending, and then advised the speakers to leave the town as soon as possible, which they did. When they left, the meeting had lasted a mere ten minutes.

10 OCTOBER 1942

Elizabeth Sheila Ferguson (16), a nanny who had been looking after the children of Lt Sandeman, RN, and his wife Eva at Seaton, Downderry, was seen walking away from their villa. She was leading one child by each hand, and all were soaked in blood. When questioned, she said that a maniac had invaded the premises and attacked Mrs Sandeman with a knife, so she had taken the children and gone away to get help. Mrs Sandeman was indeed found dead from massive stab wounds. The nanny, however, then changed her story, and said she had just returned from a walk when Mrs

Sandeman attacked her with a reaping hook, and she ran to the kitchen for a knife with which to protect herself. She was convicted of murder, but at her trial she was acquitted of the major charge and found guilty of manslaughter. Sentenced to five years, she served her full term and died soon after release.

11 OCTOBER 1817

For about three weeks, people walking along a road near Pelynt had been annoyed by an offensive smell from a nearby field. On this day, one man decided to investigate, and found what at first glance looked like the mangled carcass of a calf. To his horror, it turned out to be the partly-devoured body of a headless man of middle age. He was still clad in the tattered remains of clothing, including part of a woollen frock, as worn by stream-tinners, but there was no means of identifying him. The head was later discovered nearby. A halter used for horses was found tied to the stump of a tree about 2ft from the ground, and it was thought that he had hanged himself. His body had become putrid, and was soon discovered and torn by pigs, which had access to the field, and they had probably separated the head from the body.

When enquiries were made, it turned out that the farmer who owned the field had been approached by a man who had the appearance of a miner six weeks or so earlier, coming to the house looking for work. The farmer invited the man in to come and eat with him, but the man said that 'he should take no more in this world' and went away again. That same day a halter went missing from the stable. It was assumed that the man had probably been driven by distress and poverty to take his own life. An inquest was held, but failed to establish any more information, and concluded that he had 'probably left a wife and family to lament his wretched fate'.

12 OCTOBER 1917

'Now comes another nasty blow,' the author D.H. Lawrence wrote to Lady Cynthia Asquith; 'the police have suddenly descended on the house, searched it, and delivered us a notice, to leave the area of Cornwall, by Monday [15 October] next.' Lawrence and his German wife Frieda had settled there in December 1915, staying first at the Tinners Arms at Zennor, and then renting Higher Tregerthen nearby.

At first he enjoyed living in such an isolated setting in the county, which he found 'so peaceful, so far off from the world,' and it was here that he finished his novel *Women in Love*, which was published in 1920. Nevertheless he disliked the Cornish, describing them as 'like insects gone cold, living only for money, for dirt ... they all ought to die.' (If this was his genuine opinion of the people around him, was it really such a 'nasty blow' being told he and his wife had to find somewhere else to live?) He was already a controversial figure in England; his previous novel, *The Rainbow*, published in 1915, had been banned and withdrawn from sale in Britain after the courts had found a particular chapter obscene, and he had persuaded Frieda (a close relation of Count Manfred von Richthofen, the 'Red Baron'), to leave her husband and three children to elope with him; they were married in 1914 after she had divorced her first husband.

Both were very outspoken against the war and the government, and Lawrence dreaded being called up for active service because of his tubercular condition. Mrs Lawrence made no attempt to conceal her German origins, and the sound of German folk songs could sometimes be heard coming from their house. Their presence in a place near shipping lanes where enemy submarines were inflicting heavy losses on allied ships was bitterly resented. Lawrence was warned that coast-watchers were keeping a close eye on them both, and soon afterwards the police, using their powers under the terms of the Defence of the Realm Act, called on them and ordered them to go away. One chapter of a later novel by Lawrence, *Kangaroo*, was based on the time he spent in Cornwall.

13 OCTOBER 1835

A large enclosure of pilchards was made at Newquay, but unfortunately it indirectly resulted in the loss of four lives. A boat had come into the harbour with about 1,500 barrels containing fish and the fishermen were engaged in dividing the catch up between them, when a heavy ground sea caused the rope to break. The vessel overturned, and seven men were immediately thrown beneath the waves. Four were washed back into the ship, but three were drowned, and a fourth died of apoplexy, it was reported, 'from having eaten his dinner too hastily when he heard the cry of "Fish".' One of those washed back into the boat afterwards had his arm broken by the violence of the waves as he stood with his companions lashed to the capstan. The three men who lost their lives were Thomas James and Richard and Thomas Carne, and the man who died from apoplexy was Mr Matthews.

Fishermen's cottages at Newquay, c. 1910.

14 OCTOBER 1898

The steamship *Mohegan* was sunk after hitting the Manacles off St Keverne. Built in Hull, she was purchased by the Atlantic Transport Line, which was replacing ships that had been requisitioned as troop transport vessels by the American government for use in the Spanish-American War. She had made her maiden voyage that summer as SS *Cleopatra*, sailing from London to New York. Passengers complained about the vessel's unsatisfactory condition and several defects, including serious leaks, which were blamed on hasty construction, were revealed. These were repaired before she was renamed *Mohegan* and pronounced fit to sail again.

She left Tilbury for New York on 13 October under Captain Richard Griffiths and, according to her navigational instructions, should have been sailing on a course that would take her two miles due south of Falmouth. Instead she took the wrong bearing and was seen heading for the rocks by the Coverack coastguard, which tried to send out a distress signal by firing warning rockets. It was to no avail, and she ran into Vase Rock at the Manacles. Within fifteen minutes she was almost completely submerged, and 106 of the 157 people on board perished, including Captain Griffiths, the assistant engineer William Kinley, and all the officers. Some of the survivors managed to swim ashore, and others were rescued by the Porthoustock lifeboat *Charlotte*.

Most of the bodies recovered were buried in a mass grave at St Keverne Church, where a memorial stained-glass window was given by the Atlantic Transport Line. Rumour had it that Griffiths had survived and been rescued by a lifeboat, but when taken ashore he quietly disappeared. He was thought to have been an Atlantic Transport Line shareholder, but had financial problems, and deliberately wrecked the ship so he could collect the insurance money. However, as he would have been blamed for

Leftt: *The burial of victims of the* Mohegan *in a mass grave at St Keverne.*

Below: *The steamship* Mohegan *was sunk near St Keverne in October 1898 with 106 lives lost.*

the loss of the ship, it was unlikely that he would have been able to claim any of the insurance funds himself.

15 OCTOBER 1941

Arthur Boulton, a fire watcher from Plymouth, was sent to prison for one month at Falmouth after pleading guilty to obtaining wine worth 5 guineas and £3 in cash from Thomas Sayers, manager of King's Hotel, Falmouth, on Christmas Eve 1940. He had obtained wine and cash on a cheque from Mr Sayers, saying he could not cash cheques as the bank was closed. He apologised to the court, said he was drinking a great deal at the time, and had every intention of redeeming the cheque.

Superintendent Morcumb said Boulton asked for another charge against him to be taken into consideration, as four days later he had obtained an engagement ring to the value of £3 5s on the strength of a story that he had money coming to him from Mr Summers, a jeweller. He gave the ring to a barmaid at the hotel, but on learning more she immediately returned it. At the time of his court appearance he was living with another woman at Plymouth, though he had a wife and child living elsewhere.

16 OCTOBER: Round Houses at Veryan

Veryan, on the Roseland Peninsula, is renowned for its whitewashed cob houses, with thatched conical roofs surrounded by crosses. They were thought to have been built around 1782 by the Revd Jeremiah Trist, a missionary and vicar, for his daughters, although there are five cottages altogether, and he was supposed to have had only three daughters. Each was constructed with no north side for the Devil to try and enter, and with no dark corners in which he could hide, even if he did succeed in getting through. The crosses on the top were also intended to keep him out. They were built on the edge of the village, so that if the Devil came by, he would encircle these houses but be unable to enter the village and go away, thus leaving them in peace.

17 OCTOBER 1946

Mr Justice Pilcher in the Probate Court granted Mrs Marion Brenton leave to presume that her husband Henry had died nearly eleven months earlier, on 24 November 1945. He and his wife had gone to live at Trevone after he retired from a business career in London. On the morning of 24 November he had gone for a walk, called at a tobacconist's shop, and was never seen again. His raincoat was found at the top of some high cliffs nearby, but a search for his body failed to find any further trace of him.

18 OCTOBER 1892

Jacob Kapp, a German musician, was charged at Falmouth with stealing a gold watch and chain and three lockets, valued at £20, the property of Althea Phillips, on 24 September, and a gold ring belonging to John Creser on 14 August. Mrs Phillips was the landlady with whom he had lodged in the town and Creser was a fellow lodger. He hid the articles in a chimney between the rafters and the roof. In his defence he pleaded being hard up, and needing money to get to London. The chairman said the prisoner had showed considerable skill in planning and executing the theft, and but for being seen to go accidentally to the place where he had concealed the items, he would probably have got away with his thefts. Under the circumstances the Bench could not pass a light sentence, and they ordered his imprisonment for six months on the first offence and two months on the second, both to run concurrently.

19 OCTOBER 1948

An inquest was held at Tavistock by the District Coroner, Mr G.D. Pearce, into the death of Albert Tucker (49), of Tithehall Cottage, West Taphouse, Lostwithiel. He had failed to return home after visiting Tavistock Goose Fair, and later that day his body was found in a canal in The Meadows, Tavistock. A verdict of accidental death by drowning was returned.

20 OCTOBER 1919

An accident at the Levant Mine, St Just, left thirty-one men dead. A metal connection holding two beam sections of the main engine, which carried miners up and down the shaft, gave way and the men fell down the shaft. Some men were crushed to death in the wreckage, while others survived for twenty-four hours or more, huddled against the rock face, only to die just before or just after being reached by their rescuers. A relief fund was set up for the families of those who had lost their lives. The mine was closed in 1930.

21 OCTOBER 1870

The Times reported severe gales throughout the county. Houses in several towns suffered major structural damage. A building at Camborne was struck by lightning and a number of trees were torn up by the roots. Several vessels along the coast were also affected and two small craft wrecked, but on the whole shipping was very fortunate. There was, however, one reported death, at Bude.

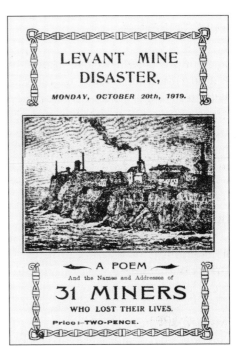

LEVANT MINE
DISASTER,
MONDAY, OCTOBER 20th, 1919.

A POEM
And the Names and Addresses of
31 MINERS
WHO LOST THEIR LIVES.
Price :- TWO-PENCE.

A pamphlet produced after the Levant Mine disaster in 1919 to help raise funds for the victims' families.

22 OCTOBER 1910

The papers reported that James Nicholas (26) was to be detained at His Majesty's pleasure for the killing of his father, Surgeon-Major James Nicholas. In July they had moved from Croydon to Cliff House, Kingsand. James the younger had returned from New Zealand only a few months earlier, having suffered from sunstroke, and was showing worrying signs of insanity. The family lived in dread of his occasional spells of violence, and feared all too accurately that it could end in tragedy. Ironically the only person who dismissed such ideas as nonsense was his father.

Early in the morning of 16 August Mrs Nicholas and daughter Yvonne were disturbed by a noise downstairs, went to investigate, and found that James had stabbed his father to death, using a Gurkha knife from a collection hanging on the drawing room wall.

When he was arrested he admitted quite calmly to having killed his father. He went on trial at Bodmin Assizes before Mr Justice Bankes on 21 October. His behaviour while in custody and in court made it clear beyond doubt that he was of unsound mind and unable to plead guilty or not guilty to either murder or manslaughter. As the law stated that no man should be convicted of a crime if members of the jury were satisfied that he was insane at the time he committed it, and as it was not considered right to put a man on trial unless he was able to comprehend exactly what was going on, the judge decided there was no point in proceeding any further. The jury, he said, ought to return a verdict that he was of unsound mind and unable to plead.

23 OCTOBER 1815

A child aged two, whose gender was not reported, lived with a family at Higher Town, near Truro, drank boiling water from a kettle which had just been removed from the fire and died in agony two days later. The *West Briton* warned its readers that the sad occurrence 'should operate as a caution to those who have the care of children to place boiling water and dangerous liquids out of their reach. A practice too common among the poor, of giving young children drink from a teapot, should be carefully avoided.'

24 OCTOBER 1822

The remains of a smuggling vessel lost during the night on the August Rocks immediately west of the Mount Pier at Mount's Bay, near Marazion, were found. Everybody on board had been killed, and the beach was covered with fragments of the wreck, and kegs of spirits. The stern of the vessel was washed on shore with the words, 'Rose, James Richards, Gweek' painted on the side. Two bodies were also recovered, one wearing a watch inscribed with the name of James Gilbert.

25 OCTOBER 1922

The Saltash Magistrates' Court charged George Lampshire of Liskeard, and Thomas Bishop and Henry Ough of St Keverne, with assaulting Constable Vincent Burrows on the evening of 21 October in the execution of his duty. Lampshire was also charged with being drunk while in charge of a motor vehicle, and another man, Robert Thorne, was summoned for obstructing the constable.

Superintendent J. Drew of the Cornwall Constabulary said that Burrows was on duty in the Square at Landrake on the Saturday. He saw Lampshire, who appeared to be drunk, going towards his car. While he was trying to start it, Lampshire collapsed across the bonnet, and Burrows said that he would not allow him to try and drive it while in such a condition. Lampshire threw off his coat and hat, and struck Burrows. A struggle took place between both men, as well as Bishop and Ough. Drew witnessed a crowd gathering, shouting at them and obviously hostile to the policeman, and Thorne tried to restrain anybody from going to get help for Burrows.

Mrs Ellen Dunn, who lived in Landrake, saw what was happening, approached them, seized one man by the shoulder and dragged him away. Walter Williams, a retired chief petty naval officer, subsequently did likewise to another of the combatants. Then Lampshire made a bid for freedom, springing into the car, and was followed by Burrows, who was attacked by Bishop. Lampshire bit the constable's finger and then got out of the car. Several people from the crowd came and pushed the car down the hill, then

Lampshire jumped back in and drove off to Liskeard. Burrows was struck in the face and chest, and kicked while he lay on the ground. He was so badly injured that he had not been back on duty since.

Lampshire and Ough pleaded guilty, Thorne and Bishop not guilty. Six witnesses, all Landrake residents, gave evidence for the prosecution. Lampshire denied that he was drunk at the time, and said that his business at Liskeard would be ruined by a police conviction. Nevertheless he was given fourteen days' imprisonment for being drunk in charge of the car, and a further month for assault. Bishop and Ough were both given fourteen days for their part in the affray, and Thorne fined £1 or fourteen days' custody in lieu.

26 OCTOBER 1899

Heavy fog resulted in two shipwrecks off the Isles of Scilly, and a near-miss for a third, within about twelve hours. At 10 p.m. on the previous night, 25 October, the full-rigged German ship *Erik Rickmers*, a 1,900-ton vessel with a cargo of rice from Akyab, struck a rock off Scilly. Distress signals were sent out and gigs launched from several different islands. All members of the crew were safely landed, but the ship, making her maiden voyage, was completely wrecked.

Six hours later the French barque *Parame*, en route from Trinidad to London, struck the remains of the *Erik Rickmers*, and capsized, though again everybody on board was saved. A little later on the same morning a large transatlantic steamer came within quarter of a mile of both wrecks and narrowly escaped running ashore.

27 OCTOBER 1790

John Chubb, aged 3 years and 9 months, died after swallowing a stone. His parents had a gravestone erected in Maker churchyard, and next to the epitaph added a full-sized carving of the fatal stone itself. The Chubbs were a tragic family, for the inscription also records the burials of John's two brothers, both named William, who died at two and three weeks respectively.

28 OCTOBER 1897

During the evening Henry Lawry, a hatter, was outside the municipal buildings at Truro where the Bishop of Truro, the Right Revd John Gott, was giving a reception in conjunction with the Diocesan Conference. Lawry was shouting offensive remarks about the bishop into the carriages bringing the guests, and several times he was asked to leave, but he persisted in making a nuisance of himself, and at length had to be removed.

The gravestone for John Chubb and his brothers in the churchyard at Maker. (© Joan Rendell)

When he appeared in court on 1 November he admitted he had been disorderly, but denied being drunk. Sergeant Eley said he was drunk and was behaving 'in a disgraceful manner'. Mr Flynn, who tried unsuccessfully to take Lawry home, could not agree Lawry was drunk, but said he seemed to be 'rather excited'. The worst thing he heard him say was, 'Mr Bishop, you haven't called the poor, the lame and the blind; you have got nobody here but the rich. You ought to have called together the poor who have no bread in their cupboards.'

Lawry said in his defence that he was 'subject to a considerable degree of excitement and natural exuberance and was consequently unable to take things as coolly as others did.' He had not gone to the Public Buildings with the intention of creating any disturbance, and did not even know the Diocesan Conference was taking place. When he saw that people were leaving, he merely took the opportunity of saying a few things. One thing which had saddened him very much was that the bishop had said that 'woman was not capable of the same degree of worship as man.' It was woman, he insisted, who 'stuck to the Saviour until the last, when others fled' and it had been cruel and grossly irreligious for the bishop to make such remarks. To laughter, he said the bishop was a round man in a square hole.

When the magistrates retired to consider the case, Lawry went on addressing everyone else left in the court, to much amusement, saying, 'We may as well pass away the time comfortably, you know.' On returning the mayor said that the case was one of the most painful which had come before the court, considering the defendant's position in town, and the fact that the magistrates were more or less his friends. He imposed a fine of 2s 6d and costs.

29 OCTOBER 1941

An egg-packing and poultry station at Liskeard belonging to E.A. Luscombe & Co. was destroyed by fire. At 4.10 p.m. it was discovered that straw in cardboard cases in a small garage made of galvanized iron was alight, and the fire quickly spread to woodwork and the beams of the roof. A car caught fire, and flames spread to the walls of the long packing shed, which was divided into an office and a working room. Papers and account books in the office section were however rescued and most of the important documents were saved.

The fire crept round the back of the building, where there was a hedge and dry bushes, and these were soon ablaze. Petrol in the garage flared up, and a thick column of black smoke shot into the air, accompanied by orange flames. Loud reports were heard as heated asbestos exploded. The cause of the outbreak was unknown, but there were no reasons to suppose it was due to enemy action.

30 OCTOBER 1916

At Falmouth Police Court, Sidney Rogers, manager of the Prince of Wales Hotel, Market Strand, was summoned for permitting drunkenness on his premises on 19 October.

Superintendent Nicholls said that at 8.50 that evening, the house was visited by Sergeant Light and Constable Hewitt. They saw between fifteen and twenty seamen in the hotel, 'and several women of doubtful character.' A sailor was leaning against the counter with a pint of beer in front of him, and when he left the counter he fell on the floor, helplessly drunk. Another seaman, obviously 'under the influence of alcohol', was acting aggressively and spoiling for a fight. At 9 p.m. when they came out of the hotel, most of the men and several of the women were very drunk.

Defending, Mr G.H. Stock said that the men were not served with liquor at the hotel, and no sooner had they come in, than the defendant ordered them out. However, the police arrived on the scene so quickly that there was not enough time to send them away. Mr Rogers said that the men were too intoxicated to ask for a drink, and he did not supply them with any. Nevertheless the Bench called it 'a disgraceful case', and fined him £10.

31 OCTOBER 1834

The clothes of a child aged two or three (gender not given) caught fire at the Peters family home in Truro, while the mother was out. One of its brothers tried to extinguish the flames by blowing on them, and an elder sibling, seeing that this was having the opposite effect, came to help by tearing the burning clothes off. Nevertheless the victim was badly burned and lingered in agony before dying three days later. Six months earlier it had had a fortunate escape when it drank a cup containing a poisonous solution which the mother had prepared for cleaning bonnets, and was only saved when speedily given an antidote.

NOVEMBER

✤

Wadebridge, where William Osborne was fined for theft on 10 November 1948.

1 NOVEMBER 1847

Thomas Greenslade, who had left his home in Cullompton, Devon, to come to Cornwall and find work on the railway, was killed. He had been found work by Mr Findlater, contractor for the new line in the Truro area, driving one of the timber wagons. After dinner, he descended a shaft which had been sunk at Buck's Head, where a tunnel was about to be built and he was interested to see what the other workmen were doing. Ten minutes later he got back into the kibble to come back to the surface. He was coming up, when the rope holding the kibble slipped off the end of the drum and jerked suddenly. He fell out, and was thrown down a depth of about five fathoms. At an inquest in the evening it was established that he had died at once from a fractured skull.

2 NOVEMBER 1953

At an inquest at St Austell, a verdict of accidental death was returned on William Pearce (80), a retired builder from Mevagissey, who had been killed in a road accident on 22 August in a head-on collision between a taxi and a car which left both drivers and four other passengers injured.

The deputy coroner, John Pethybridge, of Bodmin, conducted the inquest. The taxi driver, David Charles, had been taking three passengers from St Austell to Mevagissey. He saw a bus, which was travelling in the opposite direction, move away from the bus stop. The car, driven by John Way, went to overtake the bus, so Mr Charles pulled in to the correct side of the road and stopped. Philip Kestell, the bus driver, signalled to Mr Way to slow down or stop. The bus and car were both at a standstill on the correct sides of the road when the collision occurred.

Mr Way said he was travelling at a speed of 30–35mph. He pulled over to the right-hand side of the road behind the bus which had stopped, and saw passengers getting off. When he got within a couple of lengths of the vehicle, it started again. He could remember nothing after that, due to concussion and a blackout, and did not recall seeing any signal from the bus driver. After Mr Kestell had waved to the car behind him to stop or slow down, he realised it was not going to stop so he immediately halted the bus. At this point the car overtook him and went head-on into the taxi.

3 NOVEMBER 1884

Two men, Captain Thomas Dudley (37) and Edwin Stephens, went on trial at Exeter Assizes on a charge of murdering Richard Parker (17) in what is to date the last recorded case of cannibalism in Britain.

The 19-ton, 52ft yacht *Mignonette* was purchased at Brightlingsea, Essex, by Mr Want, who intended to go to New South Wales. As he was no sailor himself he decided to hire a crew. He engaged Dudley, Stephens, Parker and Edward Brooks, and they set sail from Falmouth on 19 May. The vessel proceeded southwards smoothly enough at first, and crossed the Equator on 17 June. However, she foundered in a storm on 5 July, about 1,600 miles from the Cape of Good Hope. All those on board escaped in a small dinghy, but within a few days they had run out of food and drinking water.

After swallowing a large amount of sea water, Parker became delirious and violent, and although already showing signs of emaciation, had to be forcibly restrained from upsetting the dinghy. On or about 25 July Dudley decided that as Parker was the youngest, and did not have a wife or children, they would have to save themselves by cutting his throat so they could eat his flesh and drink his blood – which they did.

A few days later they were spotted by the German barque *Montezuma* bound for Hamburg, which took them on board, listened to their story, and placed them under arrest. As they could not be charged with any offence committed while on foreign soil (which the German ship counted as), they were taken to Falmouth, Dudley's home town. On arrival they gave themselves up to the harbour police, were charged with murder, and granted bail. People in Falmouth were so sympathetic towards the prisoners that a public subscription was opened to meet the costs of their legal defence, and raised £200 in less than three weeks. Brooks was the youngest and judged the most innocent, and the Crown decided to use him as a witness against the others. In court they pleaded guilty and were sentenced to death on 13 December. They were taken to Holloway Gaol, to be told that the Home Secretary had successfully petitioned Her Majesty the Queen and commuted their sentences to six months' imprisonment, without hard labour.

4 NOVEMBER 1930

Alice Thomas, who lived with her husband at Trenhorne Farm near Launceston, died at Plymouth City Hospital. A few days earlier she had been admitted, ostensibly with food poisoning, but her condition gradually deteriorated over several days. Annie Hearn, who had recently befriended her and her husband William, had recently lost her sister Lydia ('Minnie') after suffering from gastric complaints. When William returned home after being at his wife's bedside, he all but accused Annie of having murdered her, as she had been taken seriously ill after they had been on a picnic together and Alice had eaten some sandwiches which Annie had prepared. 'They will blame one of us,' he warned her, 'and the blame will fall heavier on you than on me.'

A post-mortem revealed a residue of arsenic in Alice's body, and an inquest later that month returned a verdict of poisoning by person or persons unknown. The bodies of Annie's sister Minnie and her aunt Mary, who had died in 1926, were both exhumed and likewise found to contain small amounts of arsenic.

Annie was found to have fled, and after her coat and hat were found on a cliff top at Looe, it was thought she might have thrown herself over the cliffs and into the sea. However, she had in fact found lodgings in Torquay and taken a job as live-in housekeeper to a local architect under the name of Mrs Faithful. After arousing the suspicions of her employer who saw her picture in the newspaper alongside a story about her disappearance, she was traced, brought back to Cornwall and charged at Bodmin Assizes with the murders of her sister Lydia and also Alice Thomas.

The trial began on 15 June 1931. Under instruction from the judge, the jury acquitted her of both crimes as there was insufficient evidence on which to convict her. William Thomas was linked to his wife's death, but again there was no evidence with which to charge him. One juror was allegedly heard to say later that the jury believed Annie and William might have acted together in murdering Alice. The case remains unsolved to this day.

5 NOVEMBER 1960

During the afternoon Miss Doris Cross, a barmaid at the Ponsmere Hotel, Perranporth, went for a walk over the sand dunes with John Batchelor (5) (son of the hotel proprietor, Jack Batchelor) and the two family Alsatians, Prince and Carl. John had often played with the dogs at home, and sometimes used to ride on their backs. However on the walk he tripped and fell, and Carl attacked him. Joseph Laszczak, the hotel chef, heard her screaming for help, went out to see what was happening, followed the trail of footmarks in the sand and saw the dog. At first he thought it was nursing the boy, but he hit it and it retreated, but by then John had been mauled to death. A post-mortem showed that he had been attacked savagely around the head, his upper and lower jaws had been fractured, and he died from a massive haemorrhage.

At the inquest on 8 November at Truro, a sobbing Miss Cross described how the dog attacked the boy, and she tried to pull it away by its collar. Laszczak said he found it impossible to believe that the dog attacked the child, as he had seen them, and also his own littler boy, playing peacefully with it. He thought John had been injured in a fall, that the barmaid had left them together while she fetched help, and being in a hysterical condition she became confused and thought that the dog must have attacked the child. The coroner, Mr L.J. Carlyon, exempted all concerned from any blame for the tragedy, but both of the dogs were destroyed.

7 NOVEMBER 1821

A report in *The Times* on this day stated that a Mr Cock, a carpenter at 'Denham', Cornwall (research has so far failed to identify the location

Perranporth Beach, where John Batchelor was mauled to death by a family dog in 1960.

of such a place within the county), was defrauded of £31 6s by gipsies. They had told him that he was destined to obtain a treasure amounting to £4,000 or more in gold, which lay buried in a certain spot near his house. They could not indicate it more accurately, but if he could obtain the above sum and carry it around with him for a certain time, he would discover the place. Having made up the amount required, he took it to the gipsies, who performed some incantations, and then in his presence wrapped up the money in an old handkerchief. It was given back to him with the assurance that, if he neither opened it for four days, nor revealed the secret, at the end of that time he would definitely find the treasure. He departed on this assurance; but after a while, fearing the gipsy had transferred the money to her own pocket, he opened the handkerchief, and to his joy found the sum was really in his possession.

Four days later he went back to find his supposed benefactors, when one of the women told him she could do nothing for him unless he would make oath that he had done as directed. When he confessed that he had looked at the money the gipsy told him to give her the handkerchief containing the money, and to place his back against hers. When this was done she gestured violently, uttering words loudly which he did not understand. Then she returned the handkerchief to him, asked him to provide a pick and a shovel, and promised she would come to his house that night and tell him where the treasure was hidden. Mr Cock departed, having provided her with the implements for digging, and waited up the whole night, watching anxiously but in vain for the gipsy to appear. By the morning he realised he must have been duped.

Opening the handkerchief he found, to his horror, only twopence was left inside.

8 NOVEMBER 1934

Mary Young, of Fernley, Saltash, was charged at Callington with driving unlawfully and posing a danger to the public on 15 September. Mrs Kelly (74) had been standing at the rear of a trader's van at St Mellion. Mrs Young was driving towards Saltash at the time, when she saw a car coming in the opposite direction. She pulled in to let the oncoming car pass, but in the process hit and injured Mrs Kelly.

Mrs Young told the Bench that she was driving slowly in third gear at the time. She said she had pulled out to overtake a van, and as she saw another car approaching from Saltash she went back to her side and applied her brakes. The car seemed to creep forward. She did not bump into Mrs Kelly, and thought she had done no more than squeeze her slightly against the van. The car, she insisted, was almost at a standstill at the time. She felt she could not have done anything else at the time, and it was a pure accident. The Bench fined her £2 and £1 11s witnesses' fees.

9 NOVEMBER 1903

It was announced that Silvanus Trevail (52), a former Mayor of Truro and president of the Society of Architects, had been found dead. He had never been strong, and his health was further undermined by depression. On 7 November he travelled on the Cornishman Express on the Great Western Railway from Truro, having booked to St Austell to attend the funeral of a relative. Between Lostwithiel and Bodmin Road, the report of a gun was heard. When a guard went to inspect, he found Trevail's body in the lavatory with a shot through the head and a revolver lying by his side.

10 NOVEMBER 1948

William Arthur Osborne (38), a lorry driver of St Petherwick, was fined at Wadebridge for stealing five sheets of galvanized iron, part of a load which he was meant to have delivered to a farmer in the district.

11 NOVEMBER 1099

According to contemporary chroniclers (though the date has often been disputed), a great storm blew up over the lost land of Lyonesse, a country beyond Land's End, which comprised several fine cities and about 140 churches. Within a few hours the sea swept across it, submerging it beneath the waves and everybody was drowned except for one man, who rode a white horse up to high ground at Perranuthnoe before the waves could overwhelm him as well.

The Trevelyan family took the design for its coat of arms, showing a white horse rising from the waves, from this story. All that remained of the land were mountain peaks to the west, which some believe to be the Isles of Scilly. Others maintain that it is eight miles north-east of the Scillies and eighteen miles west of Land's End, while others say that it is a sunken forest in Mount's Bay, the petrified tree stumps of which are visible at low tide.

Some Christians have seen it as Cornwall's own Sodom and Gomorrah, a land of debauchery and sinful living which provoked divine wrath and ultimately destruction. Over the years people have claimed to hear the church bells of Lyonesse ringing beneath the waves, or seen the towers, domes, spires and battlements beneath the waves while standing on the cliffs at Land's End. Fishermen have also been said to find small parts of the buildings in their fishing nets.

12 NOVEMBER 1945

Edward Harris, a merchant seaman of no fixed abode, was charged at Penzance with throwing stones in Market Jew Street and Broad Street, Penzance, on 13 October. He had been found at the station one night sleeping in a railway coach, and was turned out by railway employees. Although he left the station when ordered, he soon returned and began throwing stones at the men. He pleaded not guilty, and said he had been travelling around the world the last eight years. Superintendent Peel confirmed that he was a native of Penzance who had recently returned home. He was sent to prison for fourteen days with a view to mental reports being made.

13 NOVEMBER 1882

William Bartlett (46), a foreman at Calcarrow granite works near St Blazey, was hanged by William Marwood for murdering his sixteen-day-old illegitimate daughter.

While his wife was expecting their eighth child, he had an affair with Elizabeth Wherry, the nurse who had been attending her. When they discovered that she was pregnant he sent her away, as he did not want his wife to know about their affair, and she gave birth to a daughter whom they named Emma Owen, on 4 June 1882. He promised to take care of this new arrival and said he would take her to friends so she could be nursed, but instead he strangled her, placed the body in a box and threw it down a deserted mine shaft at Lanlivery.

On 3 July he was dragged out of a large but shallow pool beside a quarry, shouting, 'Let me die.' The quarry workforce who rescued him initially thought he had been rinsing out some mining equipment and had lost his balance and fallen into the water. However, it soon became apparent that he was trying to kill himself. Once this was realised, the police began to make connections with this and the rumours that a baby had been born in the area and had suddenly disappeared.

An investigation was launched and Bartlett was questioned. His answers were initially rather evasive, and he then said that he had given a couple a lump sum to take child away, and it was being well cared for. However, five days later the box containing the child's decomposed body was found by a policeman. Bartlett was arrested, kept his silence, and pleaded not guilty when he was tried at Bodmin Assizes on 29 July. The jury could not agree on their verdict, mainly as one of their number was not fully convinced as to the identity of the body. A second trial took place on 27 October, and despite the lack of any new evidence Bartlett was found guilty and condemned to death.

14 NOVEMBER 1921

An inquest was opened into the death of Annie Black (50), a shopkeeper who ran a confectionery business at Tregonissey, St Austell, who had died on 11 November. She had been unwell for several days, vomiting and complaining of pains in her side, and died ostensibly of gastro-enteritis.

On 8 November her husband Edward, who was fifteen years her junior, disappeared from the family home. As a member of the local church choir and the Red Cross detachment, regularly attending football matches in the town and ready to assist with any injuries, he was regarded as a worthy pillar of the community. By day he had worked as an insurance agent for several years, but at the time he left he owed several customers substantial sums for the delivery of policies which later proved to be non-existent. The doctor suspected Annie Black had died from something other than natural causes, refused to issue a death certificate, informed the police, and passed stomach samples to a pathologist for analysis. At the post-mortem, small traces of arsenic were found in her body. Her death was now regarded as murder.

A nationwide hunt was mounted for Mr Black, concentrated in the North West (where he had been born and brought up) after a local butcher had received a letter from him, with a Southport postmark on the envelope, saying he had made the greatest mistake of his life in leaving home under such circumstances but insisting he was not to blame for his wife's death, and vowing he would not be brought back to St Austell alive. On 21 November he was detained in a Liverpool hotel, having tried to cut his throat as the police were forcing his locked door. After hospital treatment for severe loss of blood he was arrested, brought back to Cornwall, and in February 1922 he stood trial at Bodmin charged with murdering his wife by administering arsenic. He pleaded not guilty and denied that he had ever had any kind of poison in his possession, but the jury found otherwise, and he was sentenced to death. An appeal failed and he was hanged at Exeter on 24 March.

15 NOVEMBER 1897

A five-arch granite viaduct was being constructed at Treviddo, between Liskeard and Menheniot station, to replace an old one made of wood and stone. At about 4.10 p.m. wooden ribs were being fixed in one arch, while another had been moved into position and yet another was about to be moved thus when an accident occurred. Two labourers, William Cotton (19) and Richard Toms (32), had clambered up to the top of the rib to release the block and chain used in hauling it into place. After they had done so, the rib was held steady by a guy rope, a 4in mantilla cable. Suddenly the rope snapped, probably after being strained by a sudden gust of wind. The rib turned over, and the two men were knocked off, falling a distance of between 75ft and 80ft. Cotton landed on his head and was killed at once, but Toms was still alive when rescued. His left thigh was smashed, and he lay helpless at the foot of the viaduct, screaming in agony.

The next train from Plymouth was flagged down, and he was put on a stretcher and sent to the Liskeard Cottage Hospital. Having survived the fall for over two hours, he died at about 6.40 p.m. as he was being taken into the building.

16 NOVEMBER 1632

Sir Francis Vyvyan, Captain of St Mawes Castle, was declared by the Court of the Star Chamber 'to have practised a variety of deceptions in reference to his office,' particularly with regard to not keeping the proper number of soldiers in garrison, and misappropriating money which he had received for their wages into his own pocket. He was sentenced to be committed to the Fleet, pay a fine of £2,000 to the king, and to be removed from his office of captain. According to accounts for the Star Chamber, his fine was rescinded the following February.

17 NOVEMBER 1951

Parts of Cornwall saw exceptionally heavy rain during the afternoon and evening. The worst affected was St Erth, where the railway station was flooded as a result of the drain choking outside it. At one stage the offices and

*St Mawes
Castle.*

rooms were under 4–5in of water, with boxes containing flowers and cakes
floating around until they could be rescued and placed on the counter. Roads
at Copperhouse, Hayle, and Marazion, were also badly flooded. At Newquay,
about half an inch of rainfall was recorded, mostly during the night.

Nevertheless some people welcomed the wet weather. It had been an
exceptionally dry October, the driest month of the year, with only 1.85in of
rain, compared with 1.87in in June. The rains kept salmon in the middle and
upper reaches of the rivers, where they would be safer from the attentions of
poachers. With all the springs running again, high water would afford them
some protection and ease the problems of river-keepers and water bailiffs
during the peak spawning period, which was normally from mid-November
to mid-December.

18 NOVEMBER 1861

It was reported that Penzance and surrounding areas had a very heavy
hailstorm at around 11 a.m., lasting a quarter of an hour. 'Since the cold
weather has set in,' the papers recorded, 'the public health has been very
materially affected'. Several different epidemics were raging, with large
numbers of children hit badly by 'slow fevers', scarlatina and croup, and
many adults as well as children died as a result.

In Newlyn typhus was raging; 'these diseases have not been confined to
the poorer classes, although but few of the better-to-do people have died of
them.' It was reported that the Madron Union, the workhouse at Penzance,
had a greater number of inmates than at any point within the last seven
years, 155 as of Thursday 14 November, with several on the point of death.

19 NOVEMBER 1877

Mrs Mary Dennis, an elderly lady of Charles Street, Truro, was charged at the Truro City Police Court with neglecting to provide proper food and care for an illegitimate male child whom she had taken in to nurse. The child was eleven months old, and the mother, Mrs Emily Bray, who had been deserted by her husband, paid Mrs Dennis 4s per week to look after the child.

A quarrel with a neighbour led to information being given to the police, and when the child was removed to the workhouse, it was found to be in a terrible state of emaciation, with bones protruding through its skin. It died shortly after admission to the workhouse hospital.

After the inquest the woman was set free with a reprimand, as the coroner believed that she did not mean to kill the child. The Truro police then took the case up, and the magistrates committed the woman for trial.

20 NOVEMBER 1815

As a youth John Bassett of St Enoder had been 'increasingly wild and eccentric', and at length his behaviour became so violent that his father Robert and the rest of the family could no longer look after him at home. In 1814 he was sent to the Devon Lunatic Asylum at Exeter, and discharged the following year apparently restored to normal health. During the evening he was scolded by his mother for misconduct, flew into a rage and threatened to beat her with a stick. When two of his brothers intervened and took it away from him, he snatched up a butcher's knife in the kitchen and stabbed all three. The blade penetrated his mother's stomach and she died soon afterwards. One of the brothers was stabbed through the ribs and was in a critical condition, while the other was struck twice in the chest but less seriously injured. John fled but was pursued, 'taken and placed in strict confinement', and subsequently placed in an institution at Taunton.

In October 1834 he appeared before a Court of Inquiry at Pearce's Hotel, Truro, before a barrister, commissioner and jury, who had to judge whether he was still insane. The evidence was considered before he appeared in the courtroom, with several witnesses deposing as to his mental derangement. When he was brought in to be examined, he 'appeared greatly excited', and told the commissioner he was a blackguard and a monkey from hell. When asked his age, he said he was forty-eight, wrote the figure down on a sheet of paper, 'and challenged anyone present to add a figure which would make the amount equal to fifty thousand dollars.' After he was escorted out, the commissioner and jury concluded that he was still insane, and had been so since 1809. He was sent back to the asylum at Taunton, where he presumably remained for life.

21 NOVEMBER 1932

The appropriately-named James Etheridge Beer appeared before Truro Magistrates' Court on a charge of being drunk and disorderly at Truro on 10 November. Constable Bennetts had seen him reeling and shouting in the street, watched him fall down three times, and needed help to get him to the police station. Beer had two previous convictions, one at Penzance and one at West Penwith. He was fined £1.

22 NOVEMBER 1940

An inquest was opened on the death of William Alfred Langmaid, of Trenant, Duloe. He had died on 9 November after a collision with a motorcycle during the blackout.

Mrs Collings, a witness, said she was standing in the doorway of her house, looking towards Looe, when she saw a man walking along the road towards her house smoking a cigarette. She then saw a light from a motorcycle come around the bend and collide with him. She called her husband Richard, a gamekeeper, at 8.40 p.m. He found the motorcycle in the middle of the road, and recognised Langmaid lying nearby groaning. A girl and young man were also lying in the road, both unconscious. They were all taken to Liskeard Cottage Hospital. The motorcyclist was George Parramore (19), a wireless engineer, while Miss Libby was his pillion passenger; both of them had fractured skulls, but recovered. Langmaid died after sustaining a fracture at the base of his skull. The inquest was adjourned and concluded on 31 December.

23 NOVEMBER 1951

An inquest was held at Penzance into the death of Albert Tonkin (58), of Adelaide Street. He had been found dead on the afternoon of 20 November in his kitchen from coal gas poisoning. The coroner, John Bazeley, said he had left a note 'indicating a certain disturbance of mind.' The deceased's wife, Dorothy, had come home at 5.45 p.m., forced the back kitchen door which had been secured, and found him sitting in a chair with a gas tube near him. He had suffered from kidney disease and bronchitis for a long time, but she did not recall him ever making any suggestion that he might take his own life.

24 NOVEMBER 1787

A report in *The Times* recorded the case of a heavy storm with torrential rain in which a cottage at Kenwyn sustained severe damage. A man, his wife and their three children were all asleep inside in the same bed. The mother and two of the infants were killed instantly by the debris, while the father was badly bruised, and one child at the foot of the bed escaped unhurt. The dead were buried in one grave, at a funeral attended by a large number of people.

25 NOVEMBER 1811

Isaiah Falk Valentine, a German Jew who had long settled in England and who made his living travelling around the country selling jewellery and purchasing guineas, was murdered at Fowey.

William Wyatt, landlord of the Rose and Crown, wrote inviting him to his premises, saying he had some buttons or guineas to dispose of. Valentine promptly came down on 19 November, but Wyatt kept prevaricating, until at length this evening he took Valentine to the Broad Slip in Fowey, saying they were going to meet a Captain Best. He then robbed his unsuspecting guest of £260 and pushed him into the water. Two men nearby later testified to having heard a man exclaim repeatedly in a foreign accent, 'Oh, Mr Wyatt, for God's sake let me go.'

Wyatt deposited the money in a heap of dung on his own premises, doubtless assuming it would be safer there than anywhere else. When he walked back into his bar, a man who had seen both men together asked what had become of Mr Valentine. 'Have you not heard that he was drowned,' was the reply; 'I tried to save him, but could not.'

Wyatt was arrested and brought to trial in March 1812, found guilty of murder, and hanged at Bodmin on 1 May. The execution did not go as planned, for after the hangman had placed the noose around his neck and was about to let the drop fall, Wyatt fell off, the rope slipped on his neck, and the knot nearly came under his chin, leaving the windpipe free from pressure. The noise he made trying to breathe was heard by the spectators, and it was twenty minutes before he was killed.

26 NOVEMBER 1707

Daniel Gwin, aged about 55, died the day after a fall at his home in Falmouth. He had long been a successful businessman, his public offices including that of first agent of the Falmouth packet station, collector of the customs, then postmaster and collector of the salt duty. His rise to such positions of responsibility was regarded jealously by other local merchants, who had uncovered fraudulent dealings by the customs officers. Gwin was suspended from his duties pending an investigation, but acquitted himself well in a subsequent investigation.

However, in 1698 his opponents addressed a petition to the House of Commons complaining of abuses committed by the agent of the packet

The entrance to Fowey harbour.

service. It was found that he had been in the habit of deducting 1*s* in the pound off accounts with local tradesmen for no good reason, claiming that this was 'poundage' and he had every right to do so. Further irregularities then came to light, and when the charges against him were proved, he was dismissed from his offices and fined £10,000. Although he was able to pay the fine, it was the end of his career. He started up in trade again as a shopkeeper, and also held some position under his successor as agent of the packet service, but it was an ignominious end to what had been a successful career.

27 NOVEMBER 1632

Sir John Eliot (40), a Cornish-born Member of Parliament, died of consumption in the Tower of London. Ever since he had first been returned to Westminster as member for St Germans in 1614 he had been critical of the increasing powers of the Crown, and in 1624 he demanded that Parliament's liberties and privileges, recently curtailed by King James I, should be restored.

During the reign of King Charles I he was briefly a supporter but then a staunch opponent of the inept royal favourite, the Duke of Buckingham. He regularly spoke out against what he declared was illegal taxation, and demanded more rigorous enforcement of the laws against Roman Catholics. In February 1629, after a stormy debate of the sovereign's right to levy tonnage and poundage, the king ordered an adjournment of Parliament. The Speaker was held down forcibly in the chair while Eliot's resolutions against illegal taxation and innovations in religion were read to the House.

Sir John Eliot, the Cornish-born Parliamentarian who died of consumption while imprisoned in the Tower of London in 1632.

He and eight other members were imprisoned. When examined, he refused to answer, relying on his parliamentary privilege, and was imprisoned again. In January 1630, after he had been released, he was arrested on a charge of conspiracy of resisting the king's order.

As he refused to acknowledge the jurisdiction of the court, he was fined £2,000 and sent to the Tower until he agreed to submit, which he steadfastly refused to do. While in prison he wrote several works, including *Negotium Posterorum*, an account of the 1625 Parliament, *The Monarchie of Man*, a political treatise, and *De Jure Majestatis*, a Political Treatise of Government.

After his death his son asked for permission to move the body to St Germans but the king refused, saying, 'Let Sir John Eliot be buried in the church of that parish where he died.' Eliot was interred at St Peter's Ad Vincula Church within the Tower.

28 NOVEMBER 1821

Anthony Rowse was returning from Truro to his home at Redruth, when he was attacked by a person or persons unknown who lay in wait for him among the mine burrows and shot him dead. The people of Redruth, Gwennap and Chacewater offered a reward of £400 to anyone who could give information leading to the conviction of those responsible. Rowse's widow and six children were provided for by public subscription, but nobody was ever brought to justice for the crime.

Redruth, c. 1910.

29 NOVEMBER 1577

Cuthbert Mayne, a Roman Catholic priest, was 'examined' from dawn till dusk after being declared a traitor and sentenced to be hung, drawn and quartered. In the previous year he had become chaplain to Francis Tregian of Golden Manor, Probus.

The Bishop of Exeter, William Broadbridge, had been instructed to deal severely with Roman Catholics in the West Country. On Corpus Christi Day, 8 June 1577, with the aid of several Justices of the Peace and about a hundred armed men, the Sheriff of Cornwall, Richard Grenville, surrounded and raided Tregian's house. He arrested Mayne, wearing the waxen Agnus Dei, which was strictly prohibited under Elizabethan law, and seized his books and papers. Mayne was paraded through the villages of the county to Launceston Castle, clapped in irons and held in a filthy dungeon for three months while awaiting trial.

At the next assizes in September he was tried before Roger Manwood and Sir John Jeffreys on several charges, which included 'traitorously obtaining' a Papal bull, and publishing it at Golden, teaching the ecclesiastical authority of the Pope and denying the queen's ecclesiastical authority while in prison, and celebrating Mass in the papal manner.

After he was found guilty, Tregian was ordered to forfeit all his property and lands and sentenced to death. According to the other prisoners, on 27 November Mayne's cell was said to have become full of 'a great light'. At his examination two days later, he was told his life would be spared if he promised to swear on the Bible that he would renounce his religion and acknowledge the supremacy of Queen Elizabeth as head of the Church. He took the Bible in his hands, made the sign of the cross on it, and said, 'The queen neither ever was, nor is, nor ever shall be the head of the Church in England.' Next day he was dragged through the streets of Launceston and hanged on a gibbet in the marketplace. While still alive, his body was cut down, and he fell with such force that his eye was driven out. His severed head was placed on the castle gate, and quarters of his body were despatched to Bodmin, Tregony, Wadebridge, and Barnstaple, where he was born and raised. He was the first seminary priest to be martyred in

England, and was canonised in 1970. The Catholic Church at Launceston is named after him.

30 NOVEMBER 1898

George Still was charged at Truro Magistrates' Court by the mayor, Mr W. Rose, and Mr. W. Bullen, with embezzlement. Mr M. Bennetts prosecuted, Mr R. Dobell defended, and Mr E. Carlyon observed the case on behalf of the company, Martin, Matthews, & Co., whose affairs were in liquidation at the time. The sum mentioned in the warrant was £51, but Mr Bennetts explained that he proposed only to deal with the embezzlement of three sums, amounting to between £15 and £17.

Joseph Rogers, the liquidator of the company, said he had engaged Still as a clerk on a salary of £3 per week when employed full-time, and £1 a week when employed only on market days. His appointment was effective from the commencement of liquidation proceedings until September 1897, and he was hoping to try and dispose of the business as a going concern, in realizing stock and in collecting debts, which amounted to almost £2,000. Still was instructed to enter all receipts in the cash book, bank the money, and collect all receipts from the bank. After accounts were checked, it was found that several companies had paid money to the liquidator but not all the sums were entered in the cash book. When these irregularities were discovered, Rogers sent for Still, who sent a message that he was too busy to attend, but a further warning that if he did not come, 'it would be worse for him', made him change his mind. When the discrepancies were pointed out to him, he did not offer at first to make good the losses. After he was arrested he offered to repay everything, as long as he was given enough time. He pleaded not guilty.

At the same time he was also charged with embezzling £2 8s 6d from Hosken, Trevithick, Polkinhorn & Co., while employed by them. Shortly after leaving Martin, Matthews, & Co., he was engaged as a clerk by the second firm, also based at Truro. It was a strict rule of the company that receipts for all money received by employees were to be attached to accounts presented, the penalty for failing to do so being instant dismissal. Again, Still proved careless when it came to entering transactions in the cash book. He pleaded not guilty to this second charge. The magistrates committed him for trial, allowing him bail in £50 and sureties of £25 in each case.

DECEMBER

Housel Bay and Lizard lighthouse, the scene of a suicide pact in October 1943
that went wrong and led to a murder trial on 14 December that year.

1 DECEMBER 1650

The county commissioners were instructed to proceed with charges against Anthony Gubbs, a successful trader and former Mayor of Penzance. As a staunch Puritan, he was loyal to the Parliamentary cause in an area which was still strongly Royalist in sentiment, even though Cromwell had abolished the monarchy nearly two years earlier, and officers who regarded the king's exiled son and heir as the lawful King Charles II saw him as one of their most important foes. He claimed that he had been singled out for special treatment by Colonel Humphries and his second-in-command, Lieutenant Tyson, who were harassing his family. The climax came in January 1650 when Tyson and a band of soldiers called at his house, assaulted him, and threatened to kill him and his sons.

Gubbs was charged with aiding and abetting the Royalist rebels and thus conspiring against the government. However, no surviving documents testify to any further legal action, and it appears that any charges were dropped. He and his family were left in peace, and in 1656 he became Mayor of Penzance for a second time. He died in 1662.

2 DECEMBER 1869

General Sir Hubert Hussey Vivian was shooting pheasant on the estate of Lord Vivian at Glynn, when he was accidentally shot in the eye by a fellow guest, the Hon. Mrs Boscawen. Despite speedy medical attention, it proved impossible to save the sight of the eye.

3 DECEMBER 1904

It was reported that pilchard fishing off the south coast of Cornwall was being 'held up' by a major plague of dogfish. Up to 1,500 fishermen were being deprived, at least temporarily, of their livelihood. Such a problem had happened at least three times before in living memory. In 1875, 1882 and 1884 the Cornish coasts had been visited by shoals of the same creature, and each time there was such great destruction of nets as well as fish that all ordinary fishing had to be suspended. In 1875 they were so abundant in Mevagissey Bay for two months that fishing for herring had to be suspended. As many as 2,500 dogfish had been taken off the Cornish coast at one time, but it made no appreciable difference to the number which remained. In 1884 the prospects for pilchard fishing had been good, as shoals were appearing in record numbers at the start of the season. However, they were soon surrounded by enormous quantities of dogfish, which caused such havoc on the pilchards themselves and on the fishing fleet nets that deep-sea fishing had to be abandoned for a while.

Dogfish were not only common off Cornwall but also off Devon, Orkney, and the Shetlands. They were brown or reddish grey in colour, voracious feeders, relying mainly on smaller fish.

Mr Boulenger, the vice-president of the Zoological Society, who was in charge of the Fish and Reptile Department at the Natural History Museum, Kensington, said that charges of dynamite would kill large numbers of dogfish but destroy many others too. It was impossible trying to keep numbers down, and all the authorities and fishermen could do was wait until they abandoned that part of the coast of their own accord.

4 DECEMBER 1829

Several members of a family in the parish of St Stephens were awoken during the night by a woman's cries of 'Murder!' Some of them fetched a light and approached her bed, only to be startled by a large rat which suddenly jumped off and ran at them before escaping. The woman was covered in blood from wounds on her right shoulder and face. She said she had been woken by feeling her shoulder torn from the rodent's teeth, and tried to free herself from its grip as she screamed for help. Meanwhile the rat fixed its teeth in her cheek and held on tightly until it was disturbed by the approach of the others.

5 DECEMBER 1867

Mr Bouldon, a provision dealer, was returning home from Redruth Market in the evening when his horse was suddenly stopped. Bouldon then found himself being pulled forcefully out backwards from his cart onto the road, and was told that as long as he kept quiet he would not be injured. Three men proceeded to rob him of his watch and £19, before disappearing into the darkness. The robbery occurred when the victim was within a short distance of his home.

6 DECEMBER 1947

The Padstow lifeboat was at sea for more than eight hours overnight following reports received of an explosion off the North Cornwall coast. Boscastle coastguard station sent out an SOS during the evening, reporting a red flash followed by the sound of an explosion about four miles west of the town. A lifeboat under the command of Coxswain J.T. Murt searched from 8.20 p.m. until he was recalled on 4 a.m. on Sunday 7 December. A wide area from Tintagel Head to Carnbeak was patrolled in heavy wind and seas, but no sight or even trace of any vessel in distress was found, nor any wreckage. No boats

Trevone Bay, Padstow.

were reported missing from any of the North Cornwall harbours, and the cause of the explosion remained a mystery. One possible explanation was that a drifting mine might have struck one of the rocks rising from the sea just off the coast.

7 DECEMBER 1859

Four men were brought before St Ives magistrates, charged with assaulting a post girl a fortnight previously, and attempting to steal her letters. All were found guilty, two were committed to Bodmin Gaol for two months, and the others were sentenced to a fortnight in the town prison. This was only one of several recent cases reported, and the press remarked how disgraceful it was that the town and parish, which had a population of nearly 6,000, should have only one policeman 'to protect peaceably disposed persons from the assaults, insults and most obscene language of a great number of lads and young men who prowl about the streets, which makes it extremely dangerous for respectable females to be in the streets after dark.'

8 DECEMBER 1941

Charles Walther, a foreigner living in Bude, was brought before Stratton magistrates and charged with failing to notify a change in his registration particulars. Superintendent Mallett said on 15 November that Constable Tregaskes called at an evacuated school at Bude, when the defendant said he was employed as a French teacher. He had been asked to give lessons with a view to entering into regular employment. He made a statement in which he said he had no arrangement as to payment, but was assured he would receive something when the trial period ended and he took the job. Subsequent enquiries revealed that he was being given 2 guineas per week plus meals, and since then the money had been made up to £2 12s per week. Walther, of French nationality, though he had been born in Germany, later sent a letter to the authorities admitting that parts of the statement were untrue. He was sentenced to six months' imprisonment.

Fore Street, Bodmin, c. 1900.

9 DECEMBER 1861

An inquest was held at Bodmin Guildhall on Mr Hewett, aged about 60, who had lived in the town for a year. On the evening of 6 December he fell down very heavily on the way to his lodgings. He was taken back and put to bed, nobody thinking he was seriously injured. When the landlord looked in on him the following morning he found the man was unconscious, and he died shortly afterwards. A verdict was returned that his death was the result of the fall.

10 DECEMBER 1868

The body of Miss Martin of Lawhitton, who had been missing for a couple of days, was found in the Tamar by her youngest brother. He discovered her about seven miles below the spot where she was thought to have gone into the river. She had been suffering from depression for a while, and they were sure that she had deliberately drowned herself.

11 DECEMBER 1916

At Penzance Police Court, Martha Kewn was charged with keeping a disorderly house at New Street between 6 and 8 December, and Minnie Eva was charged with aiding and abetting her.

Chief Constable Kenyon said Mrs Kewn's husband was serving on a minesweeper at the time. Until a few months ago, she had been receiving a separation allowance for her husband and two sons who were in the navy, but this had been stopped as a result of her misconduct. For some time Mrs Eva had been lodging with her, and evidence was given 'as to what took place' on the premises. Kenyon said he hoped the Bench would deal severely with Mrs Eva, but did not know what action should be taken in the case of Mrs Kewn. It would probably be best if she went into the workhouse, as she did not have enough money to support herself and her four children at home, two girls, aged fifteen and six, and boys of ten and three and it was her own misconduct and drunken habits that had brought her to her present position. The Bench sent Mrs Eva to prison for one month with hard labour, while the case of Mrs Kewn was adjourned for a week to see if she would go to the workhouse of her own accord. At a subsequent sitting of the Juvenile Court that day, an application was made to remove Mrs Kewn's eldest daughter from her custody, and she was placed under the care of Sister McClemence for a week, while arrangements could be made to contact her father.

12 DECEMBER 1846

A longboat from the Liverpool barque *Hope*, homeward bound from Rio de Janeiro with a cargo of guano, drifted into Mawgan Porth. It had been badly damaged off the Irish coast but continued to sail until it had to be abandoned off Fishguard Bay. Ten men in a longboat were spotted by a schooner, but a blinding snowstorm held up rescue attempts and the longboat drifted away. The crew of the schooner assumed it was empty and abandoned any further attempts at rescue, but ten men were left in the bottom, without any food or water. When the boat grounded at Mawgan Porth their bodies were discovered, having frozen to death. Its wooden stern was inscribed with their names as a memorial, and when it deteriorated beyond repair a replica was produced to mark their grave in St Mawgan churchyard.

13 DECEMBER 1953

Norman Wills (39), who farmed near Liskeard, was found face down in a stream on his farm. There was a history of suicides in Wills' family; his father had committed suicide, one brother had hanged himself, another brother shot his daughter and then himself, and a cousin had also taken his own life. Not long after this event, yet another brother shot himself. On the previous day, Wills had been fined by the magistrates for not having his accounts in

The memorial to the men who froze to death in the longboat from the Hope, on their grave in the churchyard at St Mawgan in Pydar. (© Joan Rendell)

order. At the post-mortem, the pathologist Dr Hocking thought he detected signs of manual strangulation, but the rest of the evidence pointed towards yet another in a long line of family suicides.

14 DECEMBER 1943

Flying Officer William Croft (32), station commander at Housel Bay, was put on trial at Winchester for the murder of Corporal Joan Lewis (27), a WAAF from Porthcawl who had recently been posted there. He was married with two children, but after they met at a beach party their initial friendship soon turned into a passionate affair. His pangs of conscience led him to confide in the officer in charge of the WAAFs. She told him that they must break it off at once, since it was not conducive to morale or discipline, and one of them would have to be reposted. Arrangements were made for Lewis to be moved, and she was granted a couple of days' leave before her transfer, due to take place on 16 October.

Croft could not bear the thought of being parted from her, and they resolved on a suicide pact. Joan returned to duty on 14 October and on the following day she gave the impression of being quite cheerful if resigned, and they spent the night together in a summerhouse in the garden at Housel Bay Hotel. Early on the morning of 15 October 1943 Croft shot her dead, but did not have the courage to take his own life. He was charged with murder at Helston Police Court on 16 November, and tried at Winchester Assizes on 14 December.

The defence maintained that Lewis had fired the shots as part of a suicide pact, but the prosecution alleged that it would have been physically impossible for her to have fired both shots herself. In summing up, Mr Justice Humphreys said that if Lewis had killed herself, she was guilty of

Housel Bay Hotel,
The Lizard.

suicide, but if Croft had aided and abetted the suicide, he was as guilty as if he had shot her himself. The jury took less than twenty minutes to find him guilty and he was sentenced to hang. In January 1944 his appeal was dismissed, but the sentence was reduced to life imprisonment, from which he was released a few years later.

For some years afterwards witnesses reported seeing a young woman, dressed in a WAAF uniform, apparently waiting for her lover to join her in death, sitting on a bench in the hotel gardens.

15 DECEMBER 1798

At about 4 p.m. the previous day a fire broke out on board *La Coquille*, a French frigate moored at the foot of Millbrook Lake. Fifteen minutes later an explosion shook the neighbourhood, and within a short while the whole ship was ablaze. Several men jumped into the water, some being unharmed but others had already sustained burns. By next morning the ship, still burning fiercely, had been destroyed and several men had perished.

16 DECEMBER 1753

John Thomas of Marazion (61) died and was buried later that week in Gulval churchyard. On his tombstone is the design of a skull and crossbones, and above it the inscription 'WANT EXCELL'. The motif of a skull and crossbones is often seen on Cornish tombstones, and though Thomas was a well-respected man who died peacefully in his bed, a rumour has persisted that he may have been a pirate.

17 DECEMBER 1963

Russell Pascoe (24), an odd-job man and Dennis John Whitty (22), an employee at Truro gas works, who lived at Kenwyn Hill caravan site, on the outskirts of Truro, were both hanged for the murder of Garfield Rowe (64), a recluse who lived at Nanjarrow, an isolated farmhouse in the Constantine area.

Rowe's body, covered in blood, was seen in the yard by a neighbour on the morning of 15 August and reported to the police. Suspicion fell on oth men, and it was proved that they had robbed the premises although y failed to find any large sums of money, fleeing with just £4 in cash. rtheless they had killed Rowe in order to prevent him from testifying t them. He had severe head injuries, his throat had been cut, and he ral stab wounds.

r trial, which opened under Mr Justice Thesiger at Bodmin ber, each prisoner tried to put the blame on the other. Dr

Dennis John Whitty and Russell Pascoe, who were hanged for the murder of Garfield Rowe. (© Devon & Cornwall Constabulary)

Hocking, who had examined Rowe's body, thought Whitty was 'almost a little weasel of a man', and had probably planned the attack, while Pascoe, though two years older, was 'a simple lad, easily led'. The defence produced evidence that Whitty suffered from epilepsy, hysteria and a tendency to have blackouts, though there was no proof that he had a fit on the night of the murder. They pressed for an acquittal on the murder charge and a verdict of manslaughter. Nevertheless on 2 November, after four and a half hours, the jury found them both guilty and sentenced them to death.

An appeal was launched, but the sentence was upheld. Pascoe was hanged at Bristol while Whitty went to the gallows at Winchester, having celebrated his twenty-fourth birthday the day before. It proved to be the penultimate murder case on the British mainland which resulted in the guilty man (or men) being executed.

18 DECEMBER 1840

An inquest was held at Truro into the death of Master Fowler (6), son of a labourer, who had an accident in the house and set his clothes alight while his parents were out. In spite of repeated cautions recently given to families about the danger of fire, the coroner said that this was the eighth inquest he had held on children burnt to death within the last fortnight. Such fires were often caused by small children adding dry furze, which was highly combustible, to the fire during their parents' absence. These children normally wore cotton clothes, even in winter, and these were much more inflammable than woollen garments, which their parents were constantly urged to buy instead.

19 DECEMBER 1940

William John Pengelly, of Chacewater, pleaded guilty at West Powder Sessions to the theft of eggs belonging to Samuel Oatey, also of Chacewater. After thefts had been reported a watch on the farm was kept by police, and the defendant came from a field in which there were fowls and marked eggs. He produced two marked eggs from his pocket. Mr R. Frank said the defendant was of previous good character, had been in the railway service for thirty-three years, and was a disabled ex-serviceman. The case was dismissed under the First Offenders' Act on payment of 15s costs.

20 DECEMBER 1817

A heavy hailstorm fell over Cornwall, an area comprising a radius of about three miles, covering the parishes of Newlyn, Cubert, Crantock, St Columb Minor and St Dennis, 'spending its fury about Roach'. Many of the hailstones were up to 4in in diameter, 'and the sound made by their falling was like the breaking of a heavy sea.' Glass was broken in most of the houses in the area, and a partridge was found dead in a field, thought to be a victim of the storm.

St Columb Minor, screne of a freak hailstorm in 1817.

21 DECEMBER 1815

Two boys, aged about 12 and 14, were playing in a barn at Penneur, St Keverne. A loaded gun had been left lying around, the elder picked it up and fired it at the other in fun. One of the bullets entered the back of his head, 'carried off his tongue', and killed him instantly.

22 DECEMBER 1841

ster Trevelyan, aged about 15 months, was allegedly tied to a tree
vo and a half hours in front of his father's house at Penzance by
vants as a punishment. In the past he had often been made to go
food when he was naughty, and was sometimes kicked and beaten.
vas examined by the borough magistrates, and in July 1843 an
lasting seven and a half hours concluded that the parents

were said to believe that their child had been changed by fairies for an elf-child. The mayor said in conclusion that, 'as the evidence does not legally connect him with the infamous treatment of his child, we must dismiss the case.' On the next day Mr Trevelyan and his family left the town in disgrace. A crowd followed their carriage, yelling and hissing at them as they went on their way.

23 DECEMBER 1892

James Blyth (27), a labourer from Venterdon, Stoke Climsland, placed some dynamite in his mouth, lighted a fuse which he had attached to the explosive; his head was blown to pieces by the explosion and his body severely mutilated. He had been suffering for some time from consumption, and was very poor, only the previous week he had been granted relief by the Launceston guardians. A bachelor, he had lived with his brother.

24 DECEMBER 1807

Henry Trengrouse was walking near Mount's Bay when he saw the 44-gun warship *Anson* driven onto the coast during a storm. It had left Falmouth and reached Ushant, off the Breton coast, when bad weather forced it to turn back. The captain mistook the Lizard for Falmouth, and in making for land 60yds from shore the vessel overturned. Over 120 men were drowned as they could not make the short distance from the wreck to the shore because of the boiling surf.

This inspired Trengrouse to devise some form of life-saving apparatus to reduce loss of life in similar accidents. Later, while watching a firework display on Helston Green, he decided a rocket-powered line might provide the solution. His thought was that if lightweight rockets attached to ropes were put on the ships, grounded ships could help themselves by firing these rockets to the shore thus enabling the sailors to escape to the shore along the ropes.

He completed his apparatus in 1808, and a committee later reported that his method appeared the best. It was recommended that a specimen apparatus should be placed in every dockyard in the country so that all naval officers would become familiar with its methods.

25 DECEMBER: Cattle and Oxen at Christmas

Legend has it that all the oxen and cows at a farm in the parish of St Germans, and also in parts of West Devon, can be found on their knees when the clock strikes midnight on Christmas Eve. A man living on the edge of St Stephen's Down, near Launceston, in the late eighteenth century, wanted to test the veracity of this belief. Shortly before midnight he and several others stood watching the beasts in their stalls, and observed the two eldest oxen fall upon their knees at the exact time, as they made 'a cruel moan, like Christian creatures'.

26 DECEMBER 1853

James Holman (29), a labourer at Crowan, appeared to be running for help from his house when he met two of the sons of his neighbour, Mr Roberts. He asked if their father was at home, as he had just come back to find that his wife Philippa, who was seven months pregnant, had been murdered. When they found Mr Roberts both men went back to the cottage together, where they found Mrs Holman's body under the grate, her face covered with blood and ashes. When her face was washed, several deep wounds were found over the temple and nose. There was blood on the sleeve of Holman's coat and trousers, and some was scattered over the room.

On the day of the post-mortem, 29 December, a surgeon asked Holman if he kept a hatchet on the premises. He denied doing so, but nobody believed him. Two days later a well beside the cottage was searched and drained, and a bloodstained hatchet was recovered. Only then did he admit to having committed the murder. He said that when he accused her of being drunk, as she so often was, she threw a fire hook at him, he pushed her, and she fell into the fireplace. However he did not offer any explanation for the wounds which he had evidently inflicted on her. He was charged with wilful murder, found guilty at his trial at Bodmin in March and hanged at the gaol on 3 April 1854.

27 DECEMBER 1798

It was reported that at about 10 p.m. during the previous evening Humphrey Glynn, a Customs officer attached to the boat stationed at Cawsand, was shot dead by a party of smugglers.

The boat in which he was killed was commanded by Ambrose Bowden who, with the deceased and three other officers, went to apprehend the crew of a very large smuggling cutter from Polperro, *Lottery*. Skippered by Richard Oliver, she had sailed from Guernsey a few days before Christmas, laden with a cargo of spirits and tobacco, part of which was to be unloaded at Penlee. She was south-west of Penlee Point lying at anchor and just going to put her ʾargo into boats then alongside her for the purpose of landing it.

ʾVhen Mr Bowden was within about a hundred yards of the vessel, one ʾ men on board the latter called out, 'Keep off or I will fire into you.' ʾ said he was on a king's boat and a revenue boat, and dared them to ʾhis time they were within 20yds of each other, and the smugglers ʾn a second time to keep away. They then fired point blank at the ʾt three times. Glynn was shot in the head and died immediately.

When his body was taken back to the ship, the surgeon examined him and found that the front of his skull had been shot away. The fire was returned and was kept up so persistently that the smugglers cut their cable and put to sea without affecting the landing of the cargo.

They knew that the Revenue men would be searching for them, so they set sail for Guernsey again and stayed away from Cornwall for five months. On their return to the county in May 1799, they were sighted off Start Point and forced to surrender. The Customs men discovered over 700 casks of gin and brandy as well as large quantities of tea, tobacco and salt aboard. Those who had been aboard at the time of Glynn's death were arrested and tried at the Old Bailey on 10 December 1800 for wilful murder on the high seas. Roger Toms was persuaded to give evidence against the others in exchange for his freedom. He named Thomas Potter as the man who fired the fatal shot. The others were acquitted, but Potter was found guilty and hanged.

28 DECEMBER 1932

William Henry Phillips, of Treworgan, Cubert, appeared at Pydar Petty Sessions, charged with theft from a neighbouring farmer. He pleaded guilty to stealing 20lb of hay, valued at 1s, from Arthur Harris of Llanfair, Cubert, on 22 December. Constable Magor, of Newquay, said he had been keeping any eye on the premises and had secreted himself in the bullocks' house that evening. He saw a man come in, and he flashed his lamp to notice Phillips with a bag of hay. Phillips dropped the bag and ran off, but witness chased him and caught him. The Chairman of the Bench, Mr S.K. Tamblyn, called it 'the most despicable theft which has come before this court,' and fined Phillips £20 or two months' imprisonment.

29 DECEMBER 1914

Francis Brady, who lived at Chacewater, was charged with using improper language in public. Giving evidence in his favour, Sergeant Oatey said that the defendant was a deeply patriotic man. He had explained that he was talking about Germany and the war, 'and his indignation ran away with him.' Nevertheless Brady was fined 2s 6d and costs.

30 DECEMBER 1941

Madelaine Janice Eddy, aged 2 years 10 months, had been suffering from whooping-cough and was prescribed regular medicine. She was left by herself for a little while after breakfast and at about 1 p.m. her mother found her asleep, which was usual as she normally did so after having been playing all morning. Then she noticed some of the medicine had gone. Little Madelaine awoke feeling drowsy and was violently sick, but then seemed better. A little later she had violent convulsions and her mother called Dr Shimmin, but by the time he arrived she was dead. The medicine had been left on the mantelpiece, and she could easily have reached it herself by standing on a chair. The mother did not think it was strong enough to need to be locked away, and she did not think her daughter would take it of her own free will as she did not like the taste. Dr Shimmin said that death was due to respiratory paralysis caused by an overdose of the medicine.

The Bull's Head, Fore Street, Callington. (© John Van der Kiste)

31 DECEMBER 1929

Maurice Furze (22), an unemployed Callington lorry driver, was charged at Callington Police Court with being drunk and disorderly in Fore Street, Callington, assaulting Constable Deacon, and wilfully damaging property at the police station. Constable Deacon had noticed the defendant outside the Bull's Head Inn, taking off his coat and offering to fight another man. As he was obviously drunk, Deacon advised him to forget it and go home. Furze refused, and instead followed the constable, offering to fight him instead. When the constable threatened to lock Furze up he became violent, struck him and struggled when he was placed under arrest. Inspector Jago said that when he was placed in a cell, Furze was still behaving violently. He tore off the seat of the closet in the cell, then smashed the cell door and window with it. Later he was overpowered and handcuffed, and spent the rest of the night the guardroom in the company of two constables. Jago said the prisoner by far the most violent man he had ever seen in a station cell in twenty Furze was given one month's hard labour on the first charge, and two on the second, fined £5 and given an order to pay the damage done 'rd charge or in default two months' further imprisonment.

HANGED AT BODMIN

Most ages are approximate

*Denotes a case mentioned in the text

DATE	NAME	AGE	CRIME
07.03.1785	Philip Randall	21	Burglary
23.03.1785	Robert Brown	33	Murder
29.07.1785	William Hill	25	Murder
07.08.1785	John Richards	25	Robbery with violence
06.04.1786	Thomas Roberts	34	Stealing sheep
26.04.1786	Francis Couth	45	Stealing sheep
10.04.1787	James Elliott	23	Burglary
20.08.1787	William Congdon	22	Stealing a watch
31.03.1791	Michael Taylor	22	Stealing a mare
31.03.1791	James Dash	23	Burglary
31.03.1791	James Symons	25	Stealing an ox
02.09.1791	Ben Willoughby	20	Murder
02.09.1791	John Taylor	26	Murder
15.09.1791	William Moyle	Not known	Killing a mare
1793	William Trewarvas	23	Murder
09.04.1795	James Frederick	33	Robbery
27.08.1795	Joseph Williams	28	Stealing sheep
1796	G.A. Safehorne	35	Murder
13.09.1798	William Howarth	24	Housebreaking
13.04.1801	William Roskilly	34	Housebreaking

25.08.1802	Richard Andrew	Not known	Forgery
02.09.1802	John Vanstone	37	Robbery
02.09.1802	William Lee	37	Robbery
1804	Joseph Strick	25	Murder
17.04.1805	John Williamson	Not known	Shopbreaking
17.04.1805	James Joyce	27	Shopbreaking
13.04.1812	Pierre Francois	24	Forgery
01.05.1812	William Wyatt	40	Murder*
1812	Frenchman, (name unknown)	30	Forgery
06.09.1813	Elizabeth Osbourne	20	Arson
31.03.1814	William Burn	21	Murder
31.03.1815	John Simms	30	Murder
24.08.1818	William Rowe	51	Stealing sheep
12.08.1820	Sarah Polgrean	37	Murder*
05.09.1820	Michael Stephens	27	Stealing sheep*
02.04.1821	John Barnicoat	24	Murder*
02.04.1821	John Thompson	17	Murder*
10.09.1821	Nicholas Gard	42	Murder
07.04.1825	William Oxford	21	Arson
19.04.1827	James Eddy	29	Highway robbery
08.08.1828	Elizabeth Commins	22	Murder
21.08.1828	Thomas Coombe	21	Housebreaking
21.08.1834	William Hocking	57	Bestiality
30.03.1835	John Henwood	29	Murder
13.04.1840	William Lightfoot	36	Murder*
13.04.1840	James Lightfoot	23	Murder*
12.08.1844	Matthew Weeks	23	Murder*
11.08.1845	Benjamin Ellison	61	Murder
03.04.1854	James Holman	29	Murder*
¹1.08.1856	William Nevin	44	Murder
08.1862	John Doidge	28	Murder*
⁸.1878	Selina Wadge	29	Murder*
¹882	William Bartlett	46	Murder
⁾1	Valeri Giovanni	31	Murder
⁾	William Hampton	24	Murder

BIBLIOGRAPHY

BOOKS

Barton, Rita, ed., *Life in Cornwall in the Early Nineteenth Century* (Bradford Barton, 1970)
———*Life in Cornwall in the Late Nineteenth Century* (Bradford Barton, 1972)
———*Life in Cornwall in the Mid-Nineteenth Century* (Bradford Barton, 1971)
Carter, Clive, *Cornish Shipwrecks*, Vols 1 & 2 (David & Charles, 1970)
Cornwall Federation of Women's Institutes, *The Cornwall Village Book* (Cornwall Federation of Women's Institutes/Countryside Books, 1991)
Ewen, C. L'Estrange, *Witchcraft and Demonism* (Heath Cranton, 1933)
Hocking, Dr Denis, *Bodies and Crimes: A Pathologist Speaks* (Book Guild, 1992)
Holgate, Mike, *Murder and Mystery on the Great Western Railway* (Halsgrove, 2006)
Hunt, Robert, *Cornish Customs and Superstitions* (Tor Mark, nd, *c.* 1970)
Mudd, David, *Cornishmen and True* (Frank Graham, 1971)
———*The Cornish Edwardians* (Bossiney, 1982)
———*Home along Falmouth & Penryn* (Bossiney, 1980)
Oliver, S. Pasfield, *Pendennis & St Mawes: An Historical Sketch of Two Cornish Castles*, Dyllanslow Truran, 1984 (facsimile of 1875 edition)
Phillipps, K.C. ed., *The Cornish Journal of Charles Lee* (Tabb House, 1995)
Procter, Ida, *Visitors to Cornwall* (Dyllanslow Truran, 1982)
Rendell, Joan, *Cornwall, Strange but True* (Sutton, 2007)
Spence, Jack, *The Smugglers of Cawsand Bay* (Jack Spence, 2007)
Van der Kiste, John, & Sly, Nicola, *Cornish Murders* (Sutton, 2007)
Whetter, James, *Cornish Weather & Cornish People in the 17th century* (Lyfrow Trelyspen, 1991)
Williams, Michael, *Cornish Mysteries* (Bossiney, 1980)

JOURNALS AND NEWSPAPERS

Birmingham Daily Post
Bristol Mercury & Daily Post
Cornish Life
Lloyd's Weekly Newspaper
Pall Mall Gazette
Penny Illustrated Paper and Illustrated Times
Reynolds's Newspaper
The Times
Western Evening Herald
Western Morning News

Other local titles published by The History Press

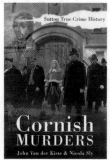

Cornish Murders
JOHN VAN DER KISTE & NICOLA SLY

Cornish Murders brings together numerous murderous tales that shocked not only the county but also made national news. They include the cases of Charlotte Dymond, whose throat was cut on Bodmin Moor in 1844; Mary Ann Dunhill, murdered in a Bude hotel in 1931; shopkeeper Albert Bateman, battered to death on his premises in Falmouth on Christmas Eve 1942; and William Rowe, brutally killed at his farm near Constantine for the sum of £4 in 1963.

978 0 7509 4707 7

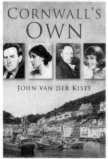

Cornwall's Own
JOHN VAN DER KISTE

Engineer and inventor Richard Trevithick, chemist Sir Humphrey Davy, artist John Opie, poet Charles Causley, opera singer Benjamin Luxon, actor John Nettles and drummer Mick Fleetwood are among well-known personalities through the ages who have been born in Cornwall. Cornwall's Own features mini-biographies of all these fascinating people and many more, and is sure to appeal to anyone interested in the county's history.

978 0 7509 5088 6

Haunted Cornwall
PAUL NEWMAN

For anyone who would like to know why Cornwall is called the most haunted place in Britain, this collection of stories of apparitions, manifestations and related supernatural incidents from around the Duchy provides the answer. The book features a gruelling exorcism at Botathan; the spectre of Annie George at the First and Last Inn at Sennen; a 'human double' clocking in for work at St Austell and a phantom stagecoach on the Mevagissey road.

978 0 7524 3668 5

Cornish Family Names
BOB RICHARDS

This handy lexicon, drawn together from exhaustive research, serves not only to give the origins and meanings of over 100 true Cornish family names but also seeks to delve into the family histories of many of the folk who have proudly borne these names right across the world down the centuries. It is packed with information and stories of many Cornish people who have left their mark and their family names in some of the farthest flung corners of the world.

978 0 7524 4976 0

Visit our website and discover thousands of other History Press books. **www.thehistorypress.co.uk**